Iron Sharpens Iron

Iron Sharpens Iron

A Discussion Guide for Twenty-First-Century Seekers

Robert P. Vande Kappelle

WIPF & STOCK · Eugene, Oregon

IRON SHARPENS IRON
A Discussion Guide for Twenty-First-Century Seekers

Wipf & Stock
An Imprint of Wipf and Stock Publishers
199 W. 8th Ave., Suite 3
Eugene, OR 97401
www.wipfandstock.com

ISBN 13: 978-1-62564-217-2

Manufactured in the U.S.A.

Bible quotations are from the *New Revised Standard Version of the Bible*, copyright
© 1989 by the Division of Christian Education of the National Council of the
Churches of Christ in the United States of America. Used by permission.

To my students at Washington & Jefferson College,
past and present, who for thirty-three years helped
create moments that were lively and true.

Special thanks to the following students in
REL 302: Global Christianity
who contributed to the 2013 sessions
that helped finalize this discussion guide:

Nicole Allison
Charlotte S. Bateman
Jamie M. Battaglia
Lauren DiGiorno
Jordan D. Easterbrook
Cameron P. Glagola
Allison H. Greene
Jeffrey D. Knopes
Annette T. Meyer
Nathan D. Michaux
Carrie L. Milliken
Wallace "Billy" A. Riley

Ferrum ferro acuitur et homo exacuit faciem amici sui.

As iron by iron is sharpened,
so a friend sharpens the wit of another.

—PROVERBS 27:17

The last experience of God is frequently
the greatest obstacle to the next experience of God.

—RICHARD ROHR

Only the senses can cure the soul
and only the soul can cure the senses.

—OSCAR WILDE

Contents

Introduction

VARIOUS SCIENTISTS—PTOLEMY, COPERNICUS, Newton, Einstein—contributed substantially to Western cosmology, thereby creating a series of paradigmatic shifts in worldview known successively as Ptolemaic, Copernican, Newtonian, and Einsteinium. When originally presented, each perspective was controversial, for it contradicted the current understanding of the cosmos. While initially resisted as heretical, each eventually became acceptable, replacing the previous mindset.

Likewise Moses, Isaiah, Plato, Aristotle, St. Paul, Origen, Augustine, Aquinas, Calvin, Schleiermacher, and Whitehead represent Western thinkers who contributed substantially to theology, helping successive generations of believers to understand God in new ways. Each emerging perspective was also controversial, for it challenged the current understanding of the divine).

There is in every human an impetus which, when nourished, seeks health and wholeness. Healthy human beings are said to go through discernible stages of growth throughout their lifetime. According to psychologist Erik Erikson, psychosocial development proceeds by critical steps. Each stage is marked by crisis, connoting not a catastrophe but a turning point, a crucial period of increased vulnerability and heightened potential. At such points achievements are won or failures occur, leaving the future to some degree better or worse but in any case, restructured. As humans grow by progressing physically, psychologically, emotionally, and even intellectually, so they undergo various stages of growth in their faith.

Out of one's individuality flows a spirituality that also yearns for growth and expression. What Erikson contributed to our understanding of the stages of psychosocial development, Jean Piaget to the stages of cognitive development, and Lawrence Kohlberg to the stages of moral development, so James Fowler did for spirituality in developing seven stages of faith, from stage zero, called "primal faith," when infants and toddlers develop (or fail to develop) a sense of safety about the universe and the divine, to a sixth stage called "universalizing faith," a rarely reached stage of those who live their lives to the full in service of others without any real fears or worries. Most people plateau at what Fowler calls the "synthetic-conventional" stage, one arising in adolescence. At this stage authority is usually placed in individuals or groups that represent one's beliefs.[1]

Like cyclists on a tandem, personality and spirituality travel together through the journey of life. Riding as one, they are deeply influenced by conditions both internal (goals, moods, desires) and external to the self. When one leans, the other leans; where one starts, the other starts; if one stops, the other stops. Though not identical, they strive to be in sync, balancing one another in profound and intimate ways.

Personality takes the lead, and where personality goes, spirituality follows, though not blindly or passively. Spirituality has its own voice, and when its desires are addressed and heeded, personality thrives. When the two disagree, they must communicate, or the consequences can be disastrous. Cooperation always enhances the ride.[2]

Like individuality, each person has a spirituality native to his or her own personality. Like personality, spirituality also yearns for growth and expression. Your spirituality, like your personality, can never be determined by someone else. It can be influenced by others, as in the case of parents and other authority figures. Ultimately, however, the choice of spirituality must be yours.

This discussion guide is grounded in the conviction that humans have the capacity to transcend conventional spirituality to a genuine and wholesome faith that is dynamic rather than static, future-oriented rather than past-oriented, and affirmed rather than passively acquired. This capacity is fueled by three principles:

1. that life is more important than death—this principle encourages us to pursue life-enhancing opportunities;

2. that whatever does not grow dies—this principle encourages us to remain open to change and newness;

3. that all truth is God's truth—this principle encourages us to remain open to truth wherever it may be found and wherever it leads.

1. Fowler's "stages of faith," including M. Scott Peck's simplified version, may be found in appendix A.

2. Individuals interested in determining (or affirming) their personality type, as revealed by the Myers Briggs Type Indicator—a device widely used in team building, organization development, business management, education, career counseling, and marriage counseling—are encouraged to examine appendix B. There they will discover how their personality type influences their learning style, spiritual journey, and theological understanding.

Andrew Walls, perhaps the leading Christian missiologist today, has compared the nature of Christian expansion to that of Islam, the world's other great missionary religion. While both have spread across the globe claiming the allegiance of diverse peoples, Islam has demonstrated more continuity in its expansion and on the whole more success in retaining allegiance. With relatively few exceptions, the areas and peoples that accepted Islam have remained Islamic ever since, whereas the ancient Christian heartland, including Egypt and Syria, is now Islamic, and the European cities once stirred by the preaching of John Knox or John Wesley are now secular, filled with empty pews and abandoned churches. While it is possible to provide social and political explanations for this loss of allegiance, Walls points to an inherent fragility in Christianity itself, a built-in vulnerability that he labels "the translation principle in Christian history."

Unlike Islam, in which the effectual hearing of the Word of Allah (recorded as the Qur'an) occurs essentially through the medium of the Arabic language and through a scripture that cannot be translated, Christianity rests on the opposite premise, on a divine act of translation known as the Incarnation: "the Word became flesh and dwelt among us" (John 1:14). In Islamic faith, God speaks to humanity in direct speech, delivered at a chosen time through God's chosen Apostle; such speech is immutable and unalterably fixed in heaven for all time. In prophetic faiths such as Judaism and Islam, God speaks; in the Christian faith, God becomes human. According to Walls, much misunderstanding has occurred due to the assumption that the Bible and the Qur'an have analogous status in the respective faiths. In fact, they are not analogous. It would be truer to say that the Qur'an is for Muslims what Christ is for Christians. "Christ, for Christians . . . is the Eternal Word of God; but Christ is Word Translated."[3]

Incarnation is translation. When God in Christ became man, divinity was translated into humanity, as though humanity were a receptor language. Translation, however, is not a precise art but a high risk business. Exact transmission of meaning from one linguistic medium to another is continually hampered by structural and cultural differences. The words of the receptor language are pre-loaded, and meanings in the source language commingle with those of the receptor to create uncharted possibilities.

In the art of translation, another point arises: language is specific to a people or an area. No one speaks "generalized language," for all language is particular. Similarly, when divinity was translated into humanity, divinity did not become generalized humanity. Divinity was embodied in

---

3. Walls, *Missionary Movement*, 27.

a particular person, in a particular locality, in a particular ethnic group, and at a particular place and time. The translation of God into humanity, whereby the sense and meaning of God was transferred, was effected under very culture-specific conditions.

This built-in vulnerability is engraved into the Christian foundational documents themselves. Whereas Islamic absolutes are fixed in a particular language, and in the conditions of a particular period of human history, the Christian revelation, including the words of Jesus himself, were transmitted not in Hebrew or Aramaic, the languages of first-century Palestinian Jews, but in translated form (Greek) in the earliest documents we have. This fragility is also linked with the essentially vernacular nature of Christian faith. For Christians, the divine Word is translatable, not once and for all, as though the translation could be captured in one time or in one place, but infinitely translatable. As Walls notes, "Christian faith must go on being translated, must continuously enter into vernacular culture and interact with it, or it withers and fades."[4] Bible translation as a process is thus both a reflection of the central act on which the Christian faith depends and of the commission that Jesus gave his disciples: "Go and make disciples of all nations" (Matt. 28:19).

As Christian faith is about translation, it is also about conversion. There is a real parallel between these processes. Translation involves the attempt to express the meaning of the source within the resources and working system of the receptor language. Something new is brought into the pre-existent language and its conventions. In translation, the original language and its system is effectively expanded, put to new use; but the translated element from the source language has also been expanded in translation. The receptor language has a dynamic of its own and takes the new material to realms never touched in the source language.

Similarly, conversion takes existing structures and turns them to new directions. Conversion is not the substitution of something new for something old or the addition of something new to something old. Rather it is the re-orientation of every aspect of humanity—culture-specific humanity—to God. By nature, then, conversion is not a single act in time, but a process. It has a beginning, but we cannot presume to posit its end. Translation, whether of the Bible to other languages, or of Christianity to other cultures and mindsets, is also a process, with a beginning but no end. Christian diversity is the necessary product of the Incarnation.

4. Walls, *Cross-Cultural Process*, 29.

Unlike Islam, whose Arabic absolutes provide cultural norms that apply across the Islamic world, Christian faith is repeatedly coming into creative interaction with new cultures, traditions, and different systems of thought. That means that Christianity's profoundest expressions are often local, vernacular, and temporal. Perhaps this is what Søren Kierkegaard, the existentialist Christian philosopher, had in mind, when he affirmed that it was "impossible to be a Christian in Christendom."

Overview: Notes for Participants

Iron Sharpens Iron is an ideal way for individuals and small groups to interact with the topics introduced in *Beyond Belief: Science, Faith, and the Value of Unknowing*, published in 2012. Like its companion text, this guide is written for those who affirm the value of lifelong spiritual growth, realize the limits of logic, and embrace the paradoxes in life. Such people see life as a mystery and often return to sacred stories and symbols, though without being confined to a theological box. This phase, identified by Fowler as "conjunctive faith," is often discovered or reached in midlife, though sooner by some. I call this stage "postcritical." If you are prepared to grow spiritually, morally, and intellectually, I encourage you to read *Beyond Belief* and embark upon the journey promoted in this guide.

Distinctive Features

Like its foundational text, this guide contains several unique features: (1) it utilizes a religious paradigm that describes one's faith story as a journey through three stages: precritical, critical, and postcritical; (2) it adheres to an understanding of scripture and of Jesus that is closer to early Jewish Christianity than to later Gentile (Hellenistic/Roman) Christianity, and (3) it affirms that science and religion (Christianity) can work cooperatively in mutually beneficial ways.

Target Audience

This book is intended for an educated audience. It targets three groups in particular: (1) those who have reached a "critical place" in their faith journey, prompted by academia, science, reason, culture, and their own experience, and who feel compelled to choose between two alternatives, either abandoning their faith or dismissing the claims of science and reason; (2) progressive individuals who will discover in this volume a framework that addresses their current theological understanding and provides impetus to move forward in their spiritual journey; and (3) conservative believers who wish to learn what "the other side" is thinking.

A Personal Note

Beyond Belief was written in response to The Outsider Test for Faith, a device that encourages individuals of various faiths to assess their truth claims from the perspective of an outsider and with the same level of skepticism they use to evaluate other religious traditions. Applying this methodology to my own religious perspective, I spent a year subjecting my religious beliefs to logical scrutiny, temporarily replacing faith presuppositions with rational and scientifically verifiable premises. This undertaking infected me with rational thinking, labeled "the philosopher's disease" by a Zen Buddhist sage. While the critical phase brings euphoria, closure, and a sense of freedom to some, my experience left me scarred, emotionally and intellectually, a condition exacerbated by my religious upbringing, my vocation, and my ordination vows.

My experiment with "the philosopher's disease" was inspired by the heroic action of Jesse William Lazear, who attended Washington & Jefferson College in the late 1880s and for whom his alma mater named the former chemistry building. At Johns Hopkins Hospital in Baltimore, where he was a medical resident and later in charge of the clinical laboratory, Lazear pursued field work and experimentation on the *Anopheles* mosquito. In June 1900 he traveled to Cuba to join Major Walter Reed on the U.S. Army Yellow Fever Commission. The mission was to grapple with this appalling plague and determine its cause. The persistence of this disease across Cuba and its periodic re-emergence along the coastlines and great river drainages of the Americas was taking countless thousands of lives. Lack of precise knowledge as to its cause and transmission had augmented yellow fever's extraordinarily high mortality rate and had given rise to quarantine regulations which constituted an impediment to regional trade. Endemic in the tropics, yellow fever imposed high humanitarian and economic costs upon the entire region. Because specialists regarded Cuba as the epicenter of the disease, the island consequently attracted considerable attention from the medical sciences. Although we now know that mosquitoes transmit the disease, this was not yet known in 1900. Some experts adhered to the theory of fomites—infections from contaminated clothing or bedding—while others believed infection to result from airborne particles.

Lazear reported to Camp Columbia, Cuba in February 1900 for duty as an acting assistant surgeon with the U. S. Army Corps stationed on the island. There he undertook bacteriological study of tropical diseases, particularly malaria and yellow fever. Lazear was the only member of the Commission who had experience with mosquito work and was consequently the most open to Cuban scientist Carlos Finlay's theory of mosquito transmission for yellow fever, a theory first developed by Finlay in 1881. By late June Lazear was beginning to grow mosquito larvae acquired from Finlay's laboratory. The project started in earnest on August 1, 1900. In a small pocket notebook Lazear noted the preparatory work of raising and infecting mosquitoes and subsequently recorded a series of eleven experimental inoculations made from the 11th to the 31st of August, the last two producing cases of full-blown yellow fever. These two positive cases that developed from mosquitoes allowed to ripen over a period of twelve days became Lazear's crucial discovery. The epidemiological pattern demonstrated a delay between the primary and secondary outbreaks of yellow fever in an epidemic and explained why Finlay's experiments had been largely unsuccessful—he had not waited long enough before inoculating his subjects.

"I rather think I am on the track of the real germ," Lazear wrote from Cuba to his wife Mabel on September 8, 1900. His experimental efforts were about to undermine yellow fever's ascendancy. Seventeen days later his own case of yellow fever, contracted a week after writing Mabel, suddenly ended the life of the thirty-four-year-old scientist. Unlike so many other yellow fever fatalities, however, this one led to a direct and highly successful assault on the disease itself. Although Lazear never directly admitted to experimenting on himself, when Reed reviewed Lazear's sketchy notations he found entries strongly suggesting Lazear's case was not accidental, as officially reported.

Unlike Lazear, who died a martyr's death and left a tangible legacy, my contribution pales by comparison, but like this pioneer, I trust that my experiment and its results can benefit those who find themselves in a quandary, disappointed by religious hopes and promises but also disillusioned by rationalistic, humanistic, naturalistic, and atheistic options. To those who find themselves in such a critical stage of faith and unable to return to precritical understanding, I hold forth an antidote that promises to renew your faith and revitalize your hope. Such fulfillment beckons in the phase known as "secondary naiveté," the postcritical stage in one's spiritual journey.

The differences between precritical, critical, and postcritical are profound. The precritical phase is a state in which people accept ("believe") as true whatever is told them by significant authority figures in their lives. For some this state is short-lived; for others, it can last a lifetime. *Beyond Belief* describes the journey from precritical to critical understanding, intellectually and theologically. There I explain the contours of the critical stage in ways that epitomize that phase, depicting religious concepts logically and rationally: Jesus is a Jewish holy man; scripture is human wisdom; God is transpersonal; eternal life is a present reality; and resurrection is spiritual metaphor.

Postcritical understanding would be less dogmatic—yes, rationality can be dogmatic—more tolerant, and open. In this phase Jesus is conceived as human and divine; scripture as humanly written yet divinely inspired; God as transpersonal and personal; eternal life as both present and future reality; and resurrection as comprising metaphorical and nonmetaphorical qualities. The polarities are symbolic, representing truths, but not necessarily factual. Whereas critical thinking leads to religious skepticism and withdrawal from religious activity, postcritical believers participate in religious rituals as meaningful but optional. They hear ancient biblical stories as "true" and recite the creeds sincerely while knowing them as not literally true. That distinction is what separates postcritical from precritical understanding. While practitioners in both phases exhibit similarities, speaking and even worshiping alike, the differences are profound, making it virtually impossible for someone who has embraced critical and then postcritical thinking to revert to precritical understanding.

Note to Participants

Consider journaling during these next twelve weeks. To do so effectively, you will want to make time for silence and meditation. A good place to start is with your hopes and dreams. Be honest with your thoughts and feelings without ignoring your fears and repressed secrets (Swiss psychiatrist Carl Jung called this your "shadow"). Embrace all aspects of your being. Set aside the mask (Jung called it the "persona") behind which you hide from others and even from yourself. Transparency will facilitate the process of becoming healthy and whole.

Note to Leaders

This guide encourages a high degree of interaction among participants. The discussion questions are engaging and appeal to various levels of intellectual/spiritual awareness. While *Beyond Belief* contains fourteen chapters, in addition to an extensive introduction, this study may be completed in twelve segments, each *45 to 60 minutes in length*. Recommended time allotments are: (1) overview, 5 minutes; (2) discussion, 35 to 50 minutes; and (3) summary, 5 minutes. If sessions are at least *90 minutes in length*, the study may be completed in eight segments. Recommended time allotments are (1) overview, 5 to 15 minutes; (2) discussion, 60 to 80 minutes; (3) summary, 5 to 15 minutes.

Study groups may modify the twelve-session pattern by eliminating some of the sessions or by rearranging the topics to suit the needs or interests of the participants. Sessions encompassing two chapters from the text (sessions 5, 6, 10, and 11) may be expanded to cover each chapter separately, increasing the total to sixteen segments. Some groups may wish to eliminate particular topics or to rearrange their order. One possibility is to begin with the section on science and evolution (sessions 10 through 12) and then to explore the impact of evolution on other topics addressed in the guidebook.

Each session follows a fourfold pattern:

- *Getting Started* (provides an overview of each chapter/session)

- *Gaining Momentum* (provides questions for discussion or further reflection; leaders and participants may be selective in determining questions for discussion)

- *Going Deeper* (proposes a project that encourages individuals and groups to acquire greater perspective through research, reading, or by additional experience)

- *The Essentials* (a synopsis of *Beyond Belief*, listing key points from each chapter or unit)

Session 1

Examining Your Faith Journey

THIS SESSION IS BASED on the Introduction to *Beyond Belief,* which promotes a questing form of spirituality, encouraging readers to re-examine their theology and explore the underpinnings of their faith.

Getting Started

Key Question: Would you describe your faith as a belief system (primarily designed to get you to heaven), a way of life, a connection to an ecclesiastical institution, or a relationship with God? Explain your answer.

Initial Assignment: Write a short narrative that tells your spiritual journey to this point. Be prepared to share your story with others. The following exercise will help in constructing your faith journey. Using a sheet of paper laid lengthwise, do the following:

a. Draw a line from left to right in the middle of the sheet;

b. List your date of birth to the extreme left of the line and today's date to the extreme right;

c. Above the line write the dates and identification of significant events in your life (e. g. birth of a sibling, death of someone, high school graduation, higher education, engagement, wedding, birth of children, etcetera);

d. Below the line write the dates and significant events happening in the world at those times (e. g. wars, floods, calamities, financial woes, etcetera);

e. Study the timeline you have created. Can you identify those times and events that correspond to any changes in your understanding of God?

f. Share your findings with your small group or with the entire class, depending on the instructions of your leader.

American Christians seem always to be on a journey of faith. The priority given to religious faith in America is demonstrated by the great variety of utopian movements and sectarian denominations that have flourished in the North American continent. Among the driving forces in American society has been the manifestation of Christian fervency known as "Great Awakenings." Such revivals punctuate America's historical record, rooting America's hopes in religious traditionalism. Recent data concerning religious affiliation in America indicate an alarming trend occurring among all Christian denominations: religious affiliation is plummeting. But such news is not all negative, as it never is in America, for this loss in affiliation is coupled with a rise of interest in "spirituality." The decline in Christian attendance and affiliation that began decades ago—and is increasing exponentially in recent years—has a hopeful side, for it is leading many Christians to approach faith with a newfound freedom both life-giving and service driven. Some are calling this emerging movement a Fourth Great Awakening, finding here a way of faith closer to the real message of Jesus.[1]

An unexamined faith, as many Christians are discovering, may not be worth following, since it is not one's own. The author suggests a contemporary and hopeful pattern for the journey of faith, a religious paradigm that describes one's faith story as a journey through precritical, critical, and postcritical stages.

The world's great spiritual personalities—Moses, Buddha, the prophets of Israel, Jesus, Muhammad, to name a few—were considered revolutionaries and even heretics in their day. They inspired their early followers to break from tradition and update their relationships to God. On his deathbed the Buddha urged his disciples: "Do not accept what you hear by report, do not accept tradition, do not accept a statement because it is found in our books, nor because it is in accord with your belief, nor because it is the saying of your teacher. Be lamps unto yourselves." It would be difficult to heed the Buddha's sage advice without being on a faith journey.

Anyone who is growing is on a journey. If you are involved with this study guide, whether on your own or with an organized group, you are on a faith journey. While some may have difficulty seeing life as a journey

1. Ross, *Christianity After Religion.*

of any sort, let alone a journey of faith, everyone needs to get in touch with one's own story. A good place to begin in conceptualizing your faith journey is to identify your personal struggles and awakenings and to acknowledge the wisdom these mentors have shown you.

The following questions can be answered individually or in a small group. If you are part of a discussion group, gather in groups of threes or fours to reflect and share your answers.

1. What is your earliest memory or thought about God? How old were you? Where were you? Do you remember how you felt? Did you share this experience with anyone?

2. How did you think or perceive of God when you were in elementary school? In your early teenage years? In your high school years? As a young adult? Has anything changed about your concept of God? What are those changes and when did they begin to occur?

3. When was the last time you remember feeling especially close to God? Where were you? Do you remember how you felt? Did you share this experience with anyone?

4. Did you ever go through a period of spiritual doubt or confusion? Where were you? Do you remember how you felt? Did you share this experience with anyone?

5. Did you ever question God's existence? How old were you? Do you remember what caused you to question God's existence? Do you remember how you felt? Did you share this experience with anyone?

6. What is your favorite Bible verse? Why is it your favorite? When did it become important to you?

7. What is your favorite hymn? Why is it your favorite? When did it become important to you?

8. Who are some Christians you especially admire? Why do you admire them?

9. When do you sense you are closest to doing God's will in society? Support your answer.

10. If you could ask God one special question and get an immediate, direct answer, what question would it be?

Gaining Momentum

1. The first paragraph of the Introduction to *Beyond Belief* identifies some of life's "ultimate questions." What are your "big questions"? Can you think of any questions you would add to the list?

2. Do you agree with the statement (page xviii of *Beyond Belief*) that every generation benefits by reexamining its theology? If so, where does one begin or conclude such a reexamination? Should such a project be comprehensive and open-ended or be limited only to specific areas such as religious values and ethical standards?

3. If you consider yourself theologically conservative, what do you understand to be the theological agenda for your generation?

4. If you consider yourself theologically moderate or liberal, what do you understand to be the theological agenda for your generation?

5. Do you agree with the statement (page xviii of *Beyond Belief*) that "The purpose of life is to experience Life"? In your own words state what you believe the author means here. In one sentence, how would you answer the question: "what is the meaning of life"?

6. How would you prioritize the four sources of theology known as the Wesleyan Quadrilateral? Support your answer.

7. In your estimation, is there sufficient evidence that Western Christianity has evolved significantly during its history, as stated on pages xix and xx of *Beyond Belief*?

8. In your understanding, is there a significant difference between "spirituality" and "religion"? Assess Neale Donald Walsch's distinctions as found on pages xxi and xxii of *Beyond Belief*.

9. Does the Overview section raise questions you might want to address in future sessions? Is a topic missing that you would like to discuss in the future? If so, what is it?

Going Deeper

Do you find the three-stage faith journey described on pages xxiii through xxiv of *Beyond Belief* valid for you? If so, where do you find yourself currently, and how did you arrive at that stage? If not, construct an alternative paradigm that addresses the faith journey more adequately.

The Essentials: Key Points from the Introduction
of *Beyond Belief*

1. The business of religion is to address those "big questions" that never go away.

2. Every generation of believers benefits from re-examining its theology, for a stagnant theology is limited in usefulness.

3. The burning theological question of every age, "is there purpose to life?" can best be answered with the reply: "the purpose of life is to experience Life." Living life fully is its own reward, for to experience life fully is to experience God.

4. Of the four sources of authority within the Christian tradition— scripture, tradition, reason, and religious experience—subjective experience is primary, both historically and practically.

5. While some observers drive a wedge between spirituality and organized religion, affirming the benefits of the former while assailing the faults of the latter, this distinction is both unnecessary and unwise.

6. The faith story has been described as a journey through three stages: precritical (primary naiveté), critical (described as a collision between inherited beliefs and those of modernity), and postcritical understanding (secondary naiveté). Many Christians seem content to remain in a precritical (unquestioning) phase, while others enter a critical phase. Some remain frozen at this stage, becoming skeptics, agnostics, or atheists, while others move forward, finding "light" at the end of their tunnel. This third stage is both a hopeful and progressive destination corresponding to "mature faith."

Session 2

Constructing a Worldview

THIS SESSION EXAMINES CHAPTER 1 of *Beyond Belief*, a segment featuring events from the author's faith journey that helped shape his precritical worldview.

Getting Started

Key Question: As you examine the core principles that comprise your religious worldview, are these values essentially precritical (inherited), critical, or postcritical?

Initial Assignment: Which doctrines or beliefs from your religious upbringing do you consider formative and essential? Be prepared to explain your answer.

What is a worldview? A personal worldview represents an individual's total outlook on life, the collection of one's assumptions, presuppositions, or convictions about reality. The Germans call it *Weltanschauung*. Nobody is without such fundamental beliefs, and yet many people go through life unaware of their presuppositions. Viewed intellectually, worldviews represent comprehensive, intentionally thought-out life and world views. Additionally, the term refers to the framework of ideas and beliefs through which an individual, group or culture interprets the world and interacts with it. The modern study of worldviews explores feelings and ideas while trying to understand what exists inside the heads of people. An important aspect of reality is people's beliefs, whether they are true.

In this session we discuss the concept of a theological worldview, a faith-based intellectual lens viewed by its advocates as logically coherent and consistent, through which all of reality may be viewed. Theological traditions often provide worldviews for their adherents, ways to configure, prioritize, and interconnect doctrines deemed integral to particular systems of belief. The author, at the start of his career, taught at Grove City College, a denominational college associated with the Presbyterian Church. There he collaborated with a team of colleagues to produce a model of essential beliefs integral to a Reformed (Calvinist) understanding of Christian doctrine. The intention was to develop a biblical view that encompassed all of life, based on the assumption that the Bible represents a divinely revealed view of reality that accurately describes the human situation. Six themes—theology (the study of God), anthropology (the study of the human being), epistemology (the study of knowledge), cosmology (the study of the universe), society, and ethics—were identified and determined to be interrelated in particular ways to form a patterned conception of reality. This approach to knowledge and reality essentially embodies the Precritical Paradigm.

Some years after participating in this endeavor the author resumed his teaching career at Washington & Jefferson College, an autonomous secular institution. Experiences in this new setting led him to reevaluate his religious worldview. He discovered that replacing theology—the traditional starting point for faith—with biology and cosmology—the starting points for modern science—redirects the flow of influence between the categories of the worldview, giving theology a "bottom-up" rather than a "top-down" role. Acknowledging the priority of science and reason led him into a critical phase in his faith, but he felt he could not remain in this state. Finding the critical state to be a stage rather than a destination, the author discovered that the way forward is not by returning to the Precritical Paradigm but by proceeding toward the more holistic Postcritical Paradigm, a far more satisfying destination.

Gaining Momentum

1. To what extent is your religious worldview inherited? In addition to your parents, who or what else has contributed to your current worldview?

2. Does organized religion influence your search for meaning and truth? If so, what role does your church or minister play in this search?

3. How does the Bible influence your worldview?

4. Does your worldview require the concept of God? Explain your answer.

5. How would you describe God? Do you support the traditional understanding of God as personal, all-powerful, and all-knowing? What are the benefits and limitations of such a description of God?

6. What changes, if any, did you make to your worldview during your adolescence and early adulthood? What challenges jeopardized or created tension in your religious beliefs over the course of your life?

7. What is your current view or understanding of eschatology? How did you arrive at this understanding?

8. What is your view of biblical inspiration? Do you subscribe to verbal inspiration? Why or why not?

9. In light of the illustrations on pages 8 and 9 of *Beyond Belief*, should the role of theology be "top-down" or "bottom-up"? Explain your answer.

10. Which paradigm do you find more attractive, the Precritical or the Postcritical? Support your answer.

Going Deeper

Do you find the six themes of the Christian worldview and their relational configuration adequate or inadequate? If inadequate, how would you change them? Construct a model that best reflects your current worldview.

The Essentials: Key Points from Chapter 1
of *Beyond Belief*

1. The Precritical Paradigm, an outlook on life most Christians acquire during childhood, is rooted in a set of beliefs based on a literal reading of biblical passages, viewed as divinely (and verbally) inspired.

2. This set of beliefs includes a doctrine of creation (that all life is part of a providential plan shaped by a singular deity who is personal, omnipotent, all-knowing, just, and altogether good), a doctrine of salvation (a way of gaining forgiveness from sins and promise of eternal life in heaven through faith in Christ), and a doctrine of eschatology (based on the

expectation that the end of human history is near and that this consummation will be preceded by the return of Christ).

3. Throughout history Christians have constructed worldviews (sets of assumptions and fundamental beliefs based on some person's or group's theological perspective) to guide their thinking, living, and religious values. Most worldviews, often creedal in nature, exemplify values and methodologies inherent in the Precritical Paradigm.

4. At an early stage in his teaching career the author embraced the Reformed worldview, a Protestant perspective based on the teachings of John Calvin. The basic premise of this approach is that the Bible presents a coherent and consistent view of reality accurately describing the human situation. The methodological approach grants theology a "top-down" role, meaning that biblical teaching concerning God (theology) is the appropriate starting point for accurately understanding the nature of humanity (anthropology), knowledge (epistemology), the universe (cosmology), society (sociology), and ethics (morality).

5. At a later point in his teaching career the author adopted an approach that replaced theology (the traditional starting point for faith) with biology and cosmology (the starting points for modern science), granting theology a "bottom-up" rather than a "top-down" role. This new approach is compatible with the Postcritical Paradigm, a way of reading scripture and doing theology amenable to science, historical scholarship, religious pluralism, and cultural diversity.

Session 3

Rethinking Dogma

THIS SESSION EXAMINES CHAPTER 2 of *Beyond Belief*, a segment that introduces the critical phase of the author's faith journey. It considers various religious topics impacted by The Outsider Test for Faith, a device formulated by former evangelical John W. Loftus to encourage individuals of all faiths to assess truth claims from the perspective of an outsider and with the same degree of skepticism they use to evaluate other religious traditions. Applying this methodology to his own religious perspective, the author spent a year subjecting his religious beliefs to logical scrutiny, replacing faith presuppositions with rationally or scientifically verifiable premises.

Getting Started

Key Question: Which traditional Christian beliefs do you question or need to rethink?

Initial Assignment: (a) Acquaint yourself with The Outsider Test for Faith (see page 13 as well as pages xxiv and xxv of *Beyond Belief*) and evaluate its usefulness for Christians. (b) What role should doubt play in the Christian life? Be prepared to share your insights with others.

Chapter 2 of the text introduces ten controversial and potentially divisive concepts, providing a critical, scholarly, and progressive examination of these issues. They include:

- how Christians interact with other religions
- the role of apologetics and evangelism in today's world
- the doctrine of predestination

- the nature of prayer, worship, and other devotional practices

- belief in miracles

- the role of biblical prophecy

- the doctrines of heaven, hell, and the afterlife

- the doctrines of sin and salvation

- the dynamic nature of Christianity

- sectarianism and ecumenism

In many ways, a sharp and ever-widening gulf characterizes the relationship between Christian scholars and traditional lay persons. The chasm is attributed to several factors, including the assumptions and conclusions of modern scholarship as well as the convictions and needs of parishioners. Scholars seek factual knowledge, whereas laypersons seek inspiration and reassurance.[1] Not all parishioners, of course, are traditionalists, and not all scholars are progressive or open to new ways of thinking about their faith.

As a participant in this study group, where do you stand? Are you on a progressive path and therefore ready for a comprehensive reexamination of Christian dogma, or are you more of a traditionalist, seeking greater clarity, depth, and certainty on what you already believe? The latter is the apologetic task, understood classically as systematic approaches that serve to clarify, defend, and assure the veracity of traditional Christian dogma. While still valuable, the role of apologetics today has diminished, particularly for those who consider members of other faiths as equals rather than as objects of conversion.

Economist E. F. Schumacher, author of *Small Is Beautiful*, believed there are two places to find wisdom: in nature and in religious traditions. To seek wisdom in nature one should look to science, to those who love nature enough to study it. Because science explores nature, it can be a powerful source of wisdom. In most developed cultures, religion and science have teamed to offer a cosmic story that allows people to understand their universe, find meaning in it, and live out their lives with purpose. In the West, however, religion and science have been at odds since the seventeenth century. This split has been disastrous: religion has become privatized and science a tool of technology. As philosopher Alfred North Whitehead wrote: "Religion is tending to degenerate into a decent formula wherewith to embellish a comfortable life . . .

---

1. Note the comparison between these two positions outlined on page 9 of *Beyond Belief* ("A Tale of Two Paradigms").

Religion will not regain its old power until it can face change in the same spirit as does science."[2] To recover the wisdom embedded in religious traditions we must abandon unhelpful religious traditions. In the words of Meister Eckhart, the most profound mystical theologian of the West: "Only those who dare to let go can dare to reenter."

What would happen to your faith—and your perspectives, priorities, lifestyle, even your attitudes—if you took as theological starting point the reality of original goodness ("original blessing") rather than original sin? The fall-redemption spiritual tradition, also known as "the heaven-and-hell framework," has dominated Christian anthropology, theology, biblical studies, theological education, and even sociology for centuries. The fall-redemption model, based on patriarchal models that are dualistic and outdated, comprises four central elements: the afterlife, sin and forgiveness, Jesus' death for the sin of humanity, and belief.

According to this model, heaven is the goal of life, the primary reason for being Christian. Sin is the central issue in one's life, and forgiveness is the solution. Because humans are sinners, they deserve to be punished. But Jesus died for our sins, thereby making forgiveness possible. Those who affirm ("believe in") this framework and accept ("have faith in") Christ's gift of forgiveness are assured eternal life with God in heaven. The fall-redemption framework, which is closely aligned with the Precritical Paradigm, views the Christian life as centered in belief now for the sake of eternal salvation. What is most important about Jesus is not his life but his death, and belief in him is central to one's eternal salvation. The goal of life is a blessed afterlife, which can only be gained through Christ's work of salvation, received by faith and maintained through worship and the sacramental life.

Critics view the fall-redemption model as guilt-ridden and therefore as psychologically flawed, in that it tends to devalue life and deprive it of much of its vitality, joy, and goodness. This framework is also said to be based on a false and unbiblical meaning of key concepts such as salvation, sacrifice, mercy, repentance, redemption, and faith, which in the Bible are concerned with temporal safety, peace, and wellbeing and rarely refer to heaven or the afterlife. In addition, this perspective is viewed by many historians and theologians as having adversely contributed to racism, sexism, nationalism, exclusivism, and other harmful ideologies.[3]

2. Whitehead, *Science and the Modern World*, 188–89.

3. For additional information on the "heaven-and-hell framework" and how particular Christian words have lost their original meaning and power, see Marcus J.

By contrast, the creation-centered tradition, which is more ancient, emphasizes goodness, blessing, joy, creativity, play, innocence, and pleasure rather than sin and guilt, and is committed to social transformation and justice-making. Because the fall/redemption tradition considers all nature "fallen" and does not seek God in nature but inside the individual soul, it tends to ignore science or be hostile to it.

According to theologian Matthew Fox, author of *Original Blessing* and other creation-centered books: "To recover a spiritual tradition in which the goodness of creation and the study of creation matters would be to inaugurate new possibilities between spirituality and science that would shape the paradigms for culture, its institutions, and its people. These paradigms would be powerful in their capacity to transform. For if wisdom comes from nature and religious traditions, as Schumacher teaches, then what might happen if science and religious traditions agreed to birth together instead of ignoring, fighting, or rejecting one another? Is not recovering a creation-centered spirituality recovering two sources of wisdom at once, that of nature via science and that of nature via religious traditions? The creation-centered tradition seems to combine the best of both worlds in our search for wisdom today."[4]

Reconfiguring Christianity's predominant dogmatic paradigm—replacing the fall/redemption model with the creation-centered model—can make a great difference in one's faith and lifestyle.

Gaining Momentum

1. Are you satisfied with your current spiritual state? If so, how do your religious beliefs contribute to your spiritual fulfillment? If not, where are you heading spiritually, and what theological adjustments could you make to get there?

2. Are there merits to the scholarly study of the Bible, or is it better to simply accept the Bible as God's word and dispense with critical scholarly approaches?

3. Of the ten topics discussed in chapter 2 of *Beyond Belief*, did one get your attention more than the others? Discuss your answer.

4. On the whole, do you agree with the critical stance taken in this

---

Borg's *Speaking Christian*, 10–17.

4. Fox, *Original Blessing*, 11–12.

chapter? Have there been times in your life when reason "trumped" faith? What was the result? Did you find yourself falling back upon a precritical foundation, remaining in the critical phase, or moving toward a postcritical solution? If possible, illustrate your answer.

5. One of the premises of the Outsider Test for Faith is "that no one religion can lay claim to ultimate truth." Do you agree with this assessment? Support your answer.

6. If you are a Christian, do you consider yourself an exclusivist, an inclusivist, a pluralist, or something else? Support your answer.

7. Traditional Christians and Muslims are taught to believe in a literal heaven and hell. What arguments support this view? What arguments dispute this view? To what extent can we understand biblical and theological depictions of heaven and hell as symbolic of deeper realities? If so, what might these deeper realities be?

8. In his discussion on sin and salvation, (see pages 28 and 29 of *Beyond Belief*) Alistair McGrath posits various answers to the questions: "From what are we saved"? and "For what are we saved"? Which of his answers do you find most valid? Why?

9. If the nature of Christianity (in terms of its core beliefs and practices) has changed dramatically since its inception in a Jewish setting some two thousand years ago, what might Christianity look like a century from now?

10. If you were to prioritize the three qualities of the church mentioned on page 33 of *Beyond Belief* (peace, unity, and purity), what order would you give? Support your answer.

Going Deeper

Read Matthew Fox's *Original Blessing*. This book represents a paradigm shift in biblical and theological thinking, for it presents a doctrinal realignment from the prevailing fall/redemption model of spirituality to a creation-centered model of spirituality.

The Essentials: Key Points from Chapter 2
of *Beyond Belief*

1. Many Christians are becoming increasingly exposed to values and perspectives that challenge their religious beliefs and worldview, propelling them into the critical phase of their faith journey. While this stage of life can be threatening and even painful, it should be embraced, for it can lead to authentic and increasingly satisfying destinations.

2. In a pluralistic age, where competing perspectives coexist, no one religion can lay claim to ultimate truth, since religious truths are based on subjective rather than objective values. In such a climate, Christians should acquire a pluralistic stance, esteeming cultural and religious diversity while affirming their own distinctive practices, beliefs, and values.

3. Belief in miracles, a notion associated with the Precritical Paradigm, is increasingly discredited or dismissed by most "modern" people. Religionists, scientists, philosophers, and other seekers of truth should remain open to unknown possibilities in the universe, while also maintaining a critical stance toward superstition in general.

4. In our age, belief in the traditional doctrine of hell is untenable, for it is incompatible with belief in a good and loving God and it contradicts rational sensibility.

5. Traditional Christians associate the death of Jesus with God's plan for the salvation of humanity. By contrast, the first Christians would have understood the death of Jesus as representing God's alternative to the temporal ruling authorities, whether the Jewish aristocrats centered in the temple in Jerusalem or the Roman system of domination.

6. Christian dogma has evolved extensively over time. Since its inception, the nature of Christianity has changed dramatically, reinventing itself as it advanced to different cultures and continents. As a result, no bridge can be built that can enable modern Christians to read the New Testament and understand the meaning of Jesus as did the first Christians.

Session 4

Knowing and Thinking Elliptically

THIS SESSION EXAMINES CHAPTERS 3 and 4 of *Beyond Belief*, a segment that encourages placing equal value upon faith and reason. Many Christians today understand faith to mean believing to be true, often literally true, a core set of statements about God, Jesus, and the Bible. However, in the Bible and throughout most of Christian history, faith and believing were not about affirming the truth of statements. They were instead about commitment, loyalty, and allegiance, and not to a set of beliefs but to God, particularly as known in Jesus. Ancient Christians were always concerned with faithfulness and trust rather than with dogma and doctrine. Beliefs mattered, but were not central. Faith was far greater, because it affected the self at its deepest level.

Getting Started

Key Question: What roles do reason and imagination play in your theological outlook?

Initial Assignment: (a) What are the various ways of knowing discussed in chapters 3 and 4 of the text? (b) How does the approach covered in these chapters nudge readers from a "critical" to a "postcritical" way of thinking and living?

Chapter 3 examines two traditional ways of knowing: *logos* (reason) and *mythos* (myth).

Both are essential and neither is superior to the other. Although *logos* is essential to human survival, it has limitations. It cannot provide ultimate meaning or help cope with tragedy or with death. For help people turn to *mythos*.

Human beings have always been mythmakers. The reason is simple: humans seek meaning, and myths reflect human ability to have ideas and experiences that cannot be explained rationally. Humans have imagination, a faculty that produces religion and mythology and also one that enables scientists to bring new knowledge to light and to invent technology that makes us more effective. The imagination of scientists has enabled humans to travel through outer space and walk on the moon, feats that were once only possible in the realm of myth. Mythology and science both extend the scope of human beings. Like science and technology, mythology is not about opting out of this world, but about helping people to live effectively though differently in a confusing world.[1]

In the premodern world, mythology was indispensable. It was not about theology, in the modern sense, but about human experience. Premodern people thought about gods, humans, animals, and nature as inextricably bound together, subject to the same laws, and composed of the same substance. When they spoke of the divine, "they were usually thinking about an aspect of the mundane. The very existence of the gods was inseparable from that of a storm, a sea, a river, or from those powerful human emotions—love, rage, or sexual passion—that seemed momentarily to lift men and women to a different plane of existence so that they saw the world with new eyes."[2] Myths may tell stories about origins, heroes, or the gods, but they are really focused on the more elusive, puzzling, and tragic aspects of the human predicament that lie outside the grasp of *logos*. A myth, therefore, is true, not because it provides factual information, but because it is effective. If a myth works, it is valid. If it ceases to provide meaning, it has outlived its usefulness.

A myth is essentially a guide telling us what we must do in order to live more effectively. If we fail to apply myth to our own situation or make it a reality in our own lives, it will remain incomprehensible and remote. When Freud and Jung began to chart the modern quest for the soul, they instinctively turned to classical mythology to explain their insights, giving the old myths a new interpretation. There was nothing new in this, there being never a single orthodox version of a myth. As circumstances change, stories must be told differently in order to bring out their timeless truth. Social scientists note that every time humans take a major step forward,

1. Armstrong, *Short History of Myth*, 2–3.
2. Ibid., 6.

they review their mythology and make it speak to the new conditions. Such scientists also note that human nature does not change much, and that ancient myths, devised in societies profoundly different from our own, still address our most essential fears and desires.[3]

From an early date, myths were enacted in stylized ceremonies that introduced participants to a deeper dimension of existence. Myth (scriptures) and ritual (ceremonies) were inseparable. Without ritual, myths made no sense. The task of religion is to enable followers to find the sort of wisdom that helps them live creatively, peacefully, and even joyously with realities for which there are no easy explanations. Of course, religion does not work automatically. It is a practical discipline that teaches humans to discover new capacities of mind and heart.

To counter the dominant influence of *logos* in the development of modern Christianity, chapter 3 emphasizes a feature in the intellectual and spiritual climate of antiquity known as the apophatic tradition, a mystical approach that flourished during the late patristic and early medieval periods. Subjecting the mind to the heart, apophatic theologians elevated "unknowing" over "knowing," valuing "unknowing" as possibly the most reliable way of understanding what could not be known rationally. This approach, promoted to some extent by theologians such as Origen (185–254), Augustine (354–430) and more fully by Evagrius of Pontus (c. 348–99), Maximus the Confessor (c. 580–662), and Denys the Areopagite (late fifth and early sixth centuries, c. 500), points to the limits of logic and lead us to *apophasis*, the inadequacy of speech, doctrine, and reason, which fragment before the unknowability of God. Preferring emptiness to fullness, darkness to light, silence to speech, faith to reason, and mental stillness to intellectual activity, Christian apophatics (like practitioners of Zen Buddhism) discovered in this "wordless" spirituality the path to peace, union, and inner tranquility. Such a path led not to intellectual ignorance but rather to intellectual rapture, taking its practitioners beyond everyday perceptions and introducing them to another mode of seeing and knowing.

In the contemporary world this perspective seems to have much in common with the mindset known as postmodernism, a way of thinking that builds on the assumption that what we call reality is constructed by the mind, and that human understanding is interpretation rather than acquisition of accurate, objective information. From this assumption it

3. Ibid., 11.

follows that our knowledge is relative, subjective, and fallible rather than certain and absolute, and that truth is inherently ambiguous.

Chapter 4 introduces two competing models for truth: the circle and the ellipse. The circular model is based on either/or thinking, a narrowly focused way of categorizing something as true *or* false, literal *or* fanciful, revealed *or* invented. Dichotomous ways of thinking are reductionistic, in that they promote either/or answers. The elliptical model, by contrast, follows a both/and approach to reality. It is holistic and inclusive; it embraces adventure and ambiguity and finds ways to feed the imagination. Mature faith (postcritical understanding) places equal value upon faith and reason, holding the two in tension. As we noted above, this understanding does not equate faith with beliefs, doctrines, or dogmas. While it might encompass such formalities, Christian faith, historically understood, focuses less on beliefs in one's head and more on loyalty in one's heart.

Chapter 4 applies the elliptical model to five theological topics, demonstrating a both/and understanding of (1) God (near *and* far), (2) prayer (vertical *and* horizontal), (3) miracles (true *and* false), (4) revelation (words of God *and* words of man), and (5) conscience (voice of God *and* voice of man). Truth, for elliptical thinking, is dialectical. Literal, one-dimensional forms of thinking set a trap, for the structure of either/or thinking implies that the options presented exhaust all other alternatives: either the Bible is divine *or* it is human; either one believes there are proofs for God's existence *or* one is an atheist; if one religion is true, others are false, and so on. Either/or thinking, intolerant of ambiguity and uncertainty, is dissatisfied with anything less than all-or-nothing answers. It accepts only absolute answers while dismissing uncertainty as a sign of unbelief.

Gaining Momentum

Chapter 3

1. In your understanding, are "faith" and "belief" essentially similar or dissimilar concepts? Should our theological beliefs change or adjust as we mature emotionally and intellectually? What about faith? Should it remain constant through life or must it change as well?

2. Scholars suggest that religions consist of "myth and ritual." What do they mean by "myth" and what roles does mythology play in humanity's search for meaning? Are all religions ultimately mythological in nature?

3. Discuss the author's understanding of "the value of unknowing"? What is meant by "unknowing," and how is this concept different from "not knowing"?

4. What is your impression of the Christian apophatic tradition? Do you find such an approach valid today? What aspects of this tradition might you apply to your own faith journey?

5. What is postmodernism, and how might postmodern views enhance the notion that "unknowing is a way of knowing"?

Chapter 4

1. In your estimation, what did Wallace Stevens mean by the statement (see page 58 of *Beyond Belief*) that "We live in the description of a place, not in the place itself"? If "religion" is the description of the place we inhabit, what is the place itself?

2. What, for you, is the greatest benefit of understanding religious thought elliptically? How does an elliptical approach affect your view of God? Of prayer? Of miracles? Of scripture as revelation?

3. What points of correlation do you find between Kierkegaard's three levels of existence and the precritical, critical, and postcritical phases in the journey of faith?

4. Evaluate Kierkegaard's "religious stage." What benefits and what concerns do you find in his understanding of faith?

5. What did Kierkegaard mean when he stated that it is "impossible to be a Christian in Christendom"? Do you agree with his assessment?

Going Deeper

Those interested in the implications of Kierkegaard's quote about being a Christian in Christendom are encouraged to read H. Richard Niebuhr work, *Christ and Culture*. There Niebuhr creates a typology, describing five major attitudes that Christians display toward human culture. These attitudes, present in all periods of church history, can be found within all major denominations. The spectrum ranges from the extremes of (a) "Christ against Culture," a pessimistic view that rejects the world and its values as evil and leads to withdrawal from secular society, and (b) "The Christ of Culture," an optimistic view that affirms the world and its values and is exemplified in state religions or "imperial theology," to three mediating positions: (c) "Christ and Culture in Paradox," a dualistic approach that encourages Christians to be "in the world but not of it," based on the notion that religion and society are separate and competing realms; (d) "Christ above Culture," a centrist view that envisions the Church's task as purifying society, providing present hope by being the "salt and light" of the world (cf. Matthew 5:13–16); and (e) "Christ the Transformer of Culture," whereby the Church provides future hope for social renewal by focusing on the transformation of the individual.

Which of these positions most closely resembles your own? Support your answer.

The Essentials: Key Points from Chapters 3 and 4
of *Beyond Belief*

Chapter 3

1. The task of religion is to enable followers to find wisdom and live creatively with realities for which there are no easy answers. Like any skill, religion requires discipline and hard work as well as intuition and imagination. Some people become adept at religion, others become inept, and others miss the point altogether, assuming that religion can be explained solely in terms of rationality, as though it were theologically factual. Because religion by nature is experiential, the essence of Christianity is relational (faith) and not dogmatic (beliefs).

2. While religionists today equate faith with dogma, this is a fairly recent endeavor. Prior to the modern period, faith was less about beliefs in one's head and more about loyalty, allegiance, and trust in one's heart.

3. Just as there are many forms of intelligence, so there are many ways of thinking, speaking, and acquiring knowledge. Ancient Greeks affirmed two modes of thought, *logos* (reason) and *mythos* (myth). Both were essential and both were equal in value.

4. During the sixteenth and seventeenth centuries, Western people developed new kinds of civilization, governed by rationality. *Logos* achieved such spectacular results that myth was discredited and the scientific method was thought to be the only reliable means of attaining truth. As theologians began to adopt the criteria of science, the *mythoi* of Christianity were interpreted to be scientifically verifiable and forced into an alien state

of thinking. This modern rationalized interpretation of religion produced two related phenomena: fundamentalism and atheism.

5. To counter the influence of rationality in religion, some of the world's greatest theologians have devised spiritual exercises that deliberately subvert normal patterns of thought and speech to help the faithful develop mystical and intuitive forms of spirituality. Apophatic forms of Christianity, which reflect this approach, prefer ambiguity, silence, and lack of certainty to theological certainty, verbosity, and sensate forms of spirituality. Such approaches, like art, dance, and music, push beyond the frontiers of language to the realm of unknowing.

6. In the fourth and fifth centuries St. Augustine left his followers a hermeneutical legacy to guide them into the unknown future: (1) *the principle of accommodation* (indicating that God had adapted revelation to the cultural norms of the original audience and that many biblical passages should not be interpreted literally), (2) *the principle of the integrity of science* (indicating that whenever the literal meaning of scripture clashed with reliable scientific information, biblical interpreters must respect the integrity of science), and (3) *the principle of charity* (indicating that if a literal understanding of any biblical passage seemed to teach hatred, the text had to be interpreted to teach love).

Chapter 4

1. Many people today were reared in faith traditions that required blind faith and that routinely answered tough questions with dogmatic answers. This approach, described as "either/or" thinking, accepts only absolute answers and dismisses uncertainty as a sign of unbelief. This form of thinking is akin to the approach called the Precritical Paradigm.

2. A more holistic, inclusive, and dialogical approach, labeled "both/and" thinking, places equal importance on imagination and reason. This way of thinking is akin to the religious approach called the Postcritical Paradigm.

3. "Both/and" thinking, called dialectical or elliptical, is simultaneously God-affirming and world-affirming. "God," according to this perspective, is everywhere present; "prayer" is a process of being open to all that life can be and then of acting to bring that fullness to pass; "miracles" represent a way of seeing life's deeper truths; "revelation" is viewed as an early phase of an ongoing tradition; and "conscience" represents a way of acting

that transcends ethical duty, even to the point of challenging human and divine imperatives. In this sense the test of the believer is not whether one believes or even obeys but what one believes and does not believe, what one obeys and does not obey.

Session 5

Thinking Panentheistically

THIS SESSION EXAMINES CHAPTERS 5 and 6 of *Beyond Belief*, a segment that considers conceptions of God and commends panentheistic understandings of God (which view the universe as in God, yet view God as more than the universe) over personalistic understandings (which view God as somehow personal yet supernatural and therefore as separate from the universe, making God more accessible but less credible).

Getting Started

Key Question: Do you perceive God as personal, impersonal, or transpersonal?

Initial Assignment: Describe the monotheistic doctrine known as supernatural theism. What, in your experience, is the greatest evidence and therefore the greatest attractiveness of the traditional view of a providential, transcendent, divine being? What is the greatest deterrent to such a view?

Building on the contributions of depth psychology, process theology, and the insights of numerous twentieth-century religious thinkers, chapter 5 focuses on the transpersonal or superpersonal aspect of God found in many religious traditions. While the idea of a "personal God" is beneficial in that it makes God relational, the extremes of this position, such as presented in the Hebrew scriptures, raise insuperable problems for people in the modern era. Many people have trouble intellectually with anthropomorphic renderings of God and with the seeming irrationality of belief in a personal God (see page 74 of *Beyond Belief* for examples). Once we conceive of God as a person like ourselves, God becomes open to criticism. The alternatives to this view (polytheism, pantheism, henotheism, and animism), seem equally foreign. Is atheism, then, the only reasonable alternative to theism? The author disagrees, presenting panentheism (a position located between traditional theism and pantheism) as the best alternative.

Chapter 5 examines two models of God found in the biblical and Christian traditions, the "monarchical model" and the "Spirit model." The monarchical model, which portrays God as male, all-powerful, lawgiver, and judge, suggests that God is distant. Those who use this image today tend to be doctrinaire and to associate God with belief, the sort of belief that appears dogmatic and hostile toward science and modernity. The Spirit model, by contrast, is less combative, more relational and tolerant, and more accepting of uncertainty and ambiguity. This perspective has proven to be more amenable to science.

Chapter 6 examines the Christian doctrine of creation and provides both historical and current examples to demonstrate how belief in God and in an evolving creation—the universe of Darwin and Einstein—stands squarely in the tradition of faith seeking understanding. In the words of eminent biologist Theodosius Dobzhansky: "It is wrong to hold creation and evolution as mutually exclusive alternatives. I am a creationist and an evolutionist."

Many contemporary scholars build on the insights of Alfred North Whitehead, the English philosopher who popularized the concept of panentheism, characterizing God's relationship to the world as that of a "Persuasive Lover." The metaphor of love is apt, for the love relationship is the fundamental and most intimate of relationships. To view God as Lover is to argue for a vulnerable God, whose relationship to the world is persuasive rather than coercive. In such a relationship the beloved (the cosmos) flourishes, responding to the Lover by evolving, growing, and emerging as a result of being loved. As in human experience, God's unconditional love for the creation must be such as to invite the creation into ever more complex levels of being.

Those who find the notion of an evolving creation and a vulnerable God threatening to their theology might find compelling the perspective of John Schneider: "Just as in human affairs love must allow the beloved freedom to make mistakes and even fall into tragedy, so God's love for his autonomous creation must take the risk of allowing evolution to lead individuals and species to suffering, death, and extinction. Such vulnerability is not weakness but strength—the strength of love."

Gaining Momentum

Chapter 5

1. Can people worship God or even relate to God meaningfully apart from a "personal" (theistic) understanding of God? Explain your answer.

2. Do you find any merit in Haught's preference for the "whatness" of God over the "whoness" of God?

3. How helpful is Haught's notion (on page 82 of *Beyond Belief*) that religious truth be rooted in two propositions, "that our lives are embraced by mystery and . . . that this mystery is gracious"? What additions, if any, would you make?

4. Which of Borg's two biblical models for God do you find most attractive, the "monarchical" or the "spirit" model? Must we choose between them? Is there a better model?

5. Assess Spong's triune approach to God and Jesus on page 88 of *Beyond Belief*. Describe the "growing edge" in your understanding of God.

Chapter 6

1. What is your understanding of the biblical/Christian doctrine of creation? Is it compatible with the scientific hypothesis of cosmic evolution?

2. Since the doctrines of God and creation appear linked, both biblically and theologically, how might changes in our understanding of God impact our understanding of the doctrine of creation?

3. Does the biblical doctrine of creation focus primarily on origins (of the cosmos and of humans) or relationships (between humans and God, others, and themselves), and thereby with human meaning and purpose in the universe?

4. In your estimation, is it possible to be both "a creationist *and* an evolutionist," as Dobzhansky argued (see page 95 of *Beyond Belief*)? If so, explain how such a synthesis might be constructed.

5. Discuss the concept of "concurrence" and how it can help to reconcile science and religion. In your estimation, are the Book of Nature and the Book of Scripture harmonizable, or are they simply two ways to compartmentalize reality?

Going Deeper

Go online or to a local library and look more deeply into Karl Barth's presentation of God as "Totally Other" and Alfred North Whitehead's panentheistic view of God. Which view of God do you find more attractive? Why? In your opinion, does traditional theism (supernatural theism) provide a better option? Explain your answer.

The Essentials: Key Points from Chapters 5 and 6
of *Beyond Belief*

Chapter 5

1. When most Christians think of God, they have in mind a supernatural being that is sovereign in the universe, yet displays personal qualities such as intelligence, feeling, and freedom. It is doubtful whether traditional Christians would worship a God who could not be described in personal terms.

2. While attributing personal qualities to God makes God relational and accessible to humanity, the extremes of this position, as presented in the Hebrew scriptures, raise insuperable problems for people in the modern era. The notion of a God who fights wars, sends storms, heals the sick, and spares the dying is becoming irrelevant or meaningless to increasing numbers in the modern world. Once people conceive of God as a person like themselves, God becomes open to criticism.

3. To protect God, apologists and theologians maintain that personal ways of thinking should be discarded. Karl Barth's solution emphasized the otherness of God, elevating God to the level of transcendent lawgiver and judge. The price paid to safeguard God's moral reputation is high, for God becomes distant and directly unapproachable. Some apologists fear that the only alternative to supernatural theism is atheism.

4. Other alternatives exist, however, including one consistently present

in the biblical and Christian tradition. This understanding of God, known as panentheism, views God as the encompassing Spirit around and within us. According to panentheism, God is both more than the universe and yet everywhere present in the universe. This view makes it possible to be an agnostic or even an atheist regarding the God of supernatural theism and yet affirm God in the way offered by panentheism.

5. Atheists and agnostics tend to view the reality of God as problematic, since they find no unambiguous evidence in ordinary human experience for a transcendent, divine presence. However, as noted by numerous thinkers, reality cannot be limited to the five senses, for reality is far too complex to be squeezed into shallow levels of perception. Religion represents the conscious rejection of the temptation to make truth the object of human mastery.

6. Alfred North Whitehead (the English philosopher who popularized the word "panentheism") depicted religion as the ongoing quest for adventure and thereby as continuous with the universe's fifteen to twenty-billion-year-old episodes of adventure. According to Catholic scholar John Haught, a purely conserving religion, while displaying an understandable passion for order, promotes the stagnation of monotony and the suspension of life's narrative story. A truly adventurous religious spirit disrupts monotony while at the same time promising hope.

7. For Haught, there are only two major "truths" required by a genuine religious sense: our lives are embraced by mystery and this mystery is gracious. He considers all religious dogmas as derivative of these two propositions.

8. Marcus Borg identifies two primary biblical models or images of God, the "monarchical model" and the "Spirit model." These models reflect two different Christian sensibilities: the supernatural sensibility (which emphasizes God's transcendence or remoteness from the human realm and views God as all-powerful lawgiver and judge) and the natural sensibility (which views God as the ever-present, all-encompassing Spirit present both within and outside humanity). The model one adopts profoundly affects one's view of the meaning of core Christian doctrines as well as of the Christian life. While the monarchical model emphasizes estrangement, the Spirit model emphasizes relationship.

Chapter 6

1. The doctrine of creation, central to all biblical faith traditions, is not solely about origins. It also affirms the essential goodness of the world and the dependence of all things upon God for existence. The biblical doctrine represents a repudiation of metaphysical dualism (which might suggest that the creation is subject to cosmic evil) as well as a repudiation of metaphysical randomness (which might suggest that life is essentially meaningless).

2. Twenty-first-century cosmogonies (accounts of the origins of the universe) offer a choice between a universe closed to influences from God and a universe open to such influences. Within an open universe, various options exist, depending upon whether one understands the role of God to be direct (creationism) or indirect (theistic evolution). Such explanations, however, are subject to a "God of the gaps" critique. This approach searches for ways to fit God into the spaces where understanding fails, but does so selectively, as a way to explain events that yield beneficial results but not events that increase suffering and yield undesirable results.

3. While it is difficult to conceptualize how the God of the Bible can operate through evolution, the problems inherent in the notion of an "open" universe are not insuperable. Modern Christians need not choose between creation and evolution. Benjamin Warfield, a highly respected theologian contemporary with Darwin, affirmed that no statement in the Bible had to be interpreted as opposed to evolution. While contemporary theologians have put forth a variety of models to explain God's relation to creation, they agree on one thing: God is not to be understood as intervening from outside the creation to accomplish providential will but instead as interacting with every creature within the creation itself.

4. Whitehead characterized God's relation to the world as that of a "Persuasive Lover," meaning by this analogy that (a) God's love is persuasive rather than coercive and (b) that the experience of the beloved (cosmos/nature/humanity) is to flourish and grow into ever more complex levels of being.

5. The notion of a vulnerable, self-limiting God is itself biblical (see kenotic theology, particularly in Philippians 2:5–8). According to kenotic theology it is God's love, not God's power, that is almighty. Such love empowers the creation to explore and unfold its evolutionary possibilities; such love takes risks, including allowing evolution to lead individuals and species to suffering, death, and extinction; such vulnerability is not weakness but strength—the strength of love.

Session 6

Rethinking the Sacredness of Scripture

THIS SESSION EXAMINES CHAPTER 7 of *Beyond Belief*, a segment utilizing early Jewish-Christian biblical methods and perspectives harmonizing with panentheism.

Getting Started

Key Question: What role does scripture play in your life and thought, and what principles do you follow in interpreting scripture?

Initial Assignment: Most modern Christians take an integrative (both/and) approach to biblical authorship: it is both human and divine. While the author of our text endorses integrative (elliptical) thinking as a general principle, with regard to biblical authorship he argues that the Bible should viewed as a human endeavor, "the product of two faith communities" (see page 106 of *Beyond Belief*). How does he arrive at this conclusion? How do you respond to this approach?

While panentheism requires a re-examination of Christian theology in its entirety, this session considers biblical authorship. Christians have always affirmed a close relationship between God and the Bible, just as other religions affirm a close connection between the sacred and their holy scriptures. Foundational to reading the Bible is a decision about how to view its origin: does it come from God or is it a human product?

Biblical scholars suggest three broad possibilities regarding the inspiration of the Bible, to which we add a fourth as corollary:

- *verbal inspiration*—the view that every word of the Bible is divinely inspired and therefore inerrant;

- *human response to inspiration*—the view that biblical writers were witnesses to divine revelation; their words and experiences may be human but they serve as vehicles to a higher voice and a deeper reality;

- *inspired imagination*—the view that the Bible is great literature, designed to capture the imagination; though the books of the Bible contain heightened insight, their message is conditioned by historical, sociological, and cultural factors. When the Bible is studied academically, it is the third of these possibilities that scholars generally have in mind.

Corollary:

- *inspired process*—the view that scripture requires ongoing interpretation. This assertion, flowing naturally from the preceding options, recognizes that the sacredness of scripture is validated by its ability to inspire Christians in every age. Scripture, defined and finalized by the canonical process, has an open-ended quality both dynamic and alive, thereby extending the revelatory process to the present. Viewing scripture as "inspired process" safeguards the original revelation while authenticating its ongoing meaning.

Acknowledging the obvious human element in the Bible, panentheists critique the widely held assumption that the Bible is both divine and human. Viewed as an entirely human product, scripture is understood to contain the perceptions and misperceptions of two communities, those of ancient Israel and those of early Christianity. The Gospels, for example, which record the account of Jesus, are considered to reflect not static truths but rather changing theological perspectives. These texts are not the words of eyewitnesses, as has so often been claimed, but were shaped by the events of the second half of the first century, perhaps even more dramatically than the events of the time in which Jesus actually lived.

What we see in the New Testament is one grand theological story, designed to capture the imagination. Those who approach the scriptures with this understanding come to see a central feature of the Bible: its essentially narrative framework. A recent emphasis in biblical and theological scholarship is the movement known as story theology, which calls attention to the centrality of "story" in the Jewish and Christian scriptures. Story theology seeks to recapture the narrative character of scripture, for the Bible originated in story. According to biblical scholar Marcus Borg, three formational stories ("macro-stories") within the Hebrew Bible have shaped the religious imagination and understanding of both ancient Israel and the early Christian movement: (1) the exodus story, (2) the story of exile and return, and (3) the priestly story. All three stories shape the message of Jesus, the New Testament, and subsequent Christian theology.

The Bible, read precritically, emphasizes biblical infallibility, historical factuality, and moral and doctrinal absolutes. Such a way of reading scripture is becoming increasingly perplexing and nonsensical to modern believers. The Postcritical Paradigm (see page 10 of *Beyond Belief* for an overview) provides an alternative to biblical literalism; scripture should be read and interpreted historically (in its original context), metaphorically (concerned more with meaning than with fact), and sacramentally (holy insofar as it mediates the sacred). The Bible is a two-way bridge, a path to the divine and a way to connect to one's deepest self. "Like a backboard," the author concludes, "scripture is a means to an end, not an end in itself" (see page 116 of *Beyond Belief*).

Gaining Momentum

1. What do Christians generally mean when they say that the Bible is "holy"? Does the word "sacred" necessarily imply anything supernatural about the origin or nature of scripture? Explain your answer (see the discussion on pages 114 and 115 of *Beyond Belief* for additional context).

2. Do you agree with the intentions, conclusions, and methodology implied in "story theology"? What weaknesses or problems do you find in such an approach to scripture? What merits or benefits do you find in this approach?

3. What lessons from the Exodus Story can you learn about bondage in your own life? What would liberation from such bondage look and feel like?

4. What lessons from the Story of Exile and Return can you learn about your own human condition? What would return from such exile look and feel like?

5. What lessons from the Priestly Story can you learn about sin and forgiveness in your own life? Identify a particular sin in your life and describe what forgiveness from that sin might look and feel like.

6. The Postcritical Paradigm views the Bible as both metaphor and sacrament. Describe the value of a metaphorical way of reading scripture. How can such a way of understanding scripture be considered sacramental?

Going Deeper

Of the three broad possibilities regarding the inspiration of the Bible (1) verbal inspiration, (2) human response to inspiration, or (3) inspired imagination, which comes closest to your understanding? Can you suggest a better option or combination of options? Construct a short paragraph that explains your answer.

For help on this topic, consult Paul J. Achtemeier's helpful volume, *The Inspiration of Scripture: Problems and Proposals* (1980). In that book Achtemeier concludes that modern study of the Bible "has rendered obsolete the model of inspiration which understands the production of each Biblical book to be the result of the inspired work of an inspired author" (p. 104). By way of support he examines three key elements: (1) the paucity of emphasis in the scriptures about their own nature as inspired; (2) the notion that the Old and New Testaments cannot be understood if read in isolation from the communities that gave them life; and (3) the importance of the canon for understanding the formation of inspired scripture. Inspiration is clearly connected to the authority of the community, subjecting biblical authority to communal authority.

The Essentials: Key Points from Chapter 7
of *Beyond Belief*

1. A panentheistic perspective requires a re-examination of Christian theology in its entirety, including one's reading and interpretation of scripture. Such an endeavor should start with early Jewish Christian methods and perspectives that harmonize with panentheism.

2. While many Christians consider the Bible to have a divine and a human origin, this approach creates an unworkable tension, for either it is all human and all divine, which is untenable, or some parts come from God and other parts are a human product. If the latter were true, how would one determine the distinction? Such distinctions, even if they could be determined, would be ultimately subjective. Furthermore, they would not really be helpful, since it is obvious that the Bible is entirely human, the product of two ancient faith communities.

3. Every passage of scripture contains a bias. It is incumbent upon each reader of the Bible to identify that bias, to determine the intention of the ancient author or community, and to interpret the meaning of that passage into the present. There is no such thing as a noninterpretive reading of the Bible.

4. The Gospels were written not by eyewitness but thirty to sixty years after the death of Jesus. They were shaped by the hopes and beliefs of their authors or communities, perhaps more than by the events of the time in which Jesus actually lived. Seeing the Gospels in their proper historical perspective is a critical first step to biblical knowledge.

5. An enormous gap exists between the claims for Jesus made by the later church and those claims actually contained in the Bible. Even The New Testament contains an expanding theological tradition.

6. A recent movement known as story theology helps us to see a vital feature of the Bible: its essentially narrative framework. Story theology not only emphasizes the centrality of story in the biblical tradition, but also criticizes much of Christian theology and modern historical scholarship for having abandoned this feature.

7. Theology typically focuses on extracting from a story a core meaning, which is then expressed conceptually. Modern historical study of the Bible has also deemphasized the story, searching instead for the underlying history or losing the story by focusing on its fragments. In both cases, the story as story disappears.

8. The Bible largely originated in story, perpetuated by storytelling long before it became text. Unlike theology and doctrine, which address understanding and belief, stories appeal to the imagination. The great stories of the Bible serve to model the religious life rather than belief.

9. At the heart of scripture lie three formational stories that have shaped the Bible as a whole and Western religious life in particular ways. Two of the stories—the "exodus story" and the "exile and return story"—are grounded in the history of ancient Israel. The third, the "priestly story," is grounded in Israel's temple institution.

10. The exodus story, initially about bondage, incorporates the themes of liberation, journey, and destination. This account enables modern audiences to deal with these themes in existentially relevant ways.

11. The story of exile and return, though grounded in a historical experience, has psychological as well as cultural-political dimensions. It addresses situations of separation from all that is familiar and safe, including marginality and victimization. It provides hope for journeys of return.

12. The priestly story, about more than ancient temple rituals, addresses human conditions of brokenness and guilt, promoting reconciliation through forgiveness.

13. All three stories shaped the message of Jesus and subsequent Christian theology. Taken together, these three stories are holistic. The priestly story, separated from the rest, came to dominate the popular understanding of Jesus and the meaning of the Christian life, thereby producing severe distortions to the overall understanding of God, the nature of the Christian life, and the goal or end of life.

14. The Bible provides Christians their identity. When the biblical story is read literally—as though it were historically factual and morally absolute—it loses its relevance. The point is not to believe in the Bible, as though it were sacred in and of itself, but to value its metaphorical and sacramental nature. The Bible, human in nature, is sacred in status and function. As such it is a two-way bridge, a way to the divine and to our deepest self.

Session 7

Rethinking Jesus and the Gospels

THIS SESSION EXAMINES CHAPTER 8 of *Beyond Belief*, a segment that addresses the nature of the adult Jesus and his beliefs about himself and his mission. Christianity relies ultimately on two assessments: Jesus's self-understanding and the early church's conceptualizing of that self-understanding.

Getting Started

Key Questions: What did the first Christians believe about Jesus? Are the Gospels reliable eyewitness accounts?

Initial Assignment: If Jesus were to appear in our midst today, what would he want us to know about his nature and his mission?

As chapter 8 makes clear, the Jesus most Christians worship today (the second person of the Trinity) is far different from the historical Jesus. That Jesus was Jewish, and his mission focused within Judaism. As a first-century Palestinian Jew, Jesus would have viewed his mission as prophetic, announcing God's coming kingdom. In addition to his prophetic role, some scholars argue that Jesus understood himself as the central figure in the eschatological (end-time) drama. Others downplay this role, viewing Jesus as a deeply Jewish but non-eschatological figure. However we depict Jesus, whether eschatologically or noneschatologically, in every respect Jesus was a Jewish figure of his day, never intending to establish a new religion. Those who fail to understand Jesus as a Jewish figure, teaching and acting within first-century Judaism, misunderstand his person and mission.

Once we understand the Jewishness of Jesus, our next step is to study the Bible, not only the Old Testament but the New Testament as well, from a Jewish perspective. This step is vital because every biblical author was Jewish by birth, the sole exception, Luke, being a gentile proselyte to Judaism. The starting point for this understanding of scripture is the Jewish exegetical method known as *haggadic midrash*, a method that will help us understand how the New Testament writers constructed their literature. Understood as a method for writing scripture, midrash comes in three forms: Halakah, Haggadah, and Pesiqta. Halakah interprets the *law* (Torah) and its relevance to ongoing situations; Haggadah interprets a biblical *story or event* by relating it to a previous story or event in sacred history; Pesiqta refers to a *sermon or exhortation* that captures themes of the past in order to interpret them as operative in the present. According to Spong, "Midrash is the Jewish way of saying that everything to be venerated in the present must somehow be connected with a sacred moment in the past. It is the ability to rework an ancient theme in a new context. It is the affirmation of a timeless truth found in the faith journey of a people so that this truth can be experienced afresh in every generation. It is the recognition that the truth of God is not bound within the limits of time but that its eternal echoes can be and are heard anew in every generation. It is the means whereby the experience of the present can be affirmed and asserted as true inside the symbols of yesterday."[1]

Haggadic midrash, then, is the act of rereading and expanding a text in the form of a new narrative to update the existential meaning. Gospel writers, for example, less concerned with recording history and more focused on writing edifying literature, recontextualized ancient material for a new situation. The Gospels, like the rest of the New Testament, are the products of developing traditions of the early Christian communities in which they were written. Some of the events reported in the Gospels really happened and reliably represent Jesus as an historical figure, but much of the tradition is history metaphorized, meaning not literally true but representing the revised understanding of the evolving Christian communities following Easter.

The first generations of Christians, the vast majority of whom were Jewish, undoubtedly saw midrash at work in their scriptures. Later generations of Christians, who tended to be gentiles, read these Jewish antecedents in their scriptures with an anti-Jewish bias that distorted the message of these books. By the start of the second century the common

1. Spong, *Resurrection*, 8–9.

ground between Jews and Christians, once vast, became nonexistent. The gentile way of reading the New Testament became increasingly dominant, until the Jewish perspective was lost altogether.

Understanding the Jewishness of Jesus and of the New Testament has profound implications for understanding Jesus, scripture, and core Christian doctrines, including the resurrection and the hope of eternal life.

Gaining Momentum

1. A very early Christian creed declared that "Jesus is Lord." What do the assertions found on page 117 of *Beyond Belief* lead us to conclude about the meaning of that creed for early Christians?

2. Many Christians find C. S. Lewis's three options concerning Jesus (see page 117 of *Beyond Belief*) persuading. The author of *Beyond Belief* finds them to be misguided. Upon reading the chapter, do you side with Lewis or with the author on this matter? Support your answer.

3. The author argues that many Christians fail to grasp the "Jewishness of Jesus." In your estimation, what does he mean by that expression? What do biblical scholars mean when they distinguish between "the Jesus of history" and "the Christ of faith"?

4. In biblical times, the eschatological topics of divine judgment and vindication seem to have been understood as referring primarily to this-worldly events, having to do more with temporal justice and divine restitution than with heavenly or supernatural events. After reading this chapter, what views might Jesus have held on this topic?

5. In your estimation, to what extent was the biblical doctrine of resurrection impacted by Jewish eschatological expectations current in the first century?

6. In this chapter we learn that the gentile way of reading and interpreting the Gospels, a method developed during the second and third generation of Christians, was a later revisionist reading that both distorted the Gospels and fueled anti-Jewish sentiment. Why did such views develop in early Christian circles? How has this mindset influenced your past approach to Jesus and the Gospels and how is it impacting your current understanding?

Going Deeper

The term "midrash" is introduced by biblical scholars as a helpful device or approach to reading and understanding the Bible as the first Christians would have read and understood its meaning. How is this way of reading and understanding scripture helpful to contemporary Christians in their interpretation and application of the biblical text? Do you agree with Spong that Christians misunderstand the nature of the Gospels and misinterpret their portrayal of the life, death, and resurrection of Jesus when they fail to understand the role of midrash in the construction of the Gospels and the interpretation of events in the life of Jesus? Explain your answer.

For help in this task you may wish to consult Bishop Spong's book *Resurrection: Myth or Reality?* or other biblical scholarship that discusses the concept of midrash in ancient Judaism.

The Essentials: Key Points from Chapter 8
of *Beyond Belief*

1. Christianity arose as a Jewish sect; Jesus was Jewish, all the earliest leaders of Christianity were Jewish, and every book of the New Testament was written from a Jewish perspective. Jesus remained a Jew all of his life. He did not intend to establish a new religion, but saw himself as having a mission within Judaism. If we fail to understand Jesus as a Jewish figure teaching and acting within Judaism, we will misunderstand his mission.

2. When early Christians confessed "Jesus is Lord," they were not emphasizing the equality of Jesus with God, or the necessity of belief in the saving significance of Jesus' life, death, and resurrection. Rather they viewed Jesus as an extraordinary human, whose influence pointed to God's gracious rule rather than to human rule. Only later and probably by stages, did Christians come to equate Jesus with God.

3. Many Christians are unaware of the Jewishness of Jesus. This is due in part to a shift in Christianity around the end of the first century, when Christianity began severing its relation with Judaism. As the Christian movement became predominantly gentile in membership and outlook, Christians became progressively anti-Semitic. It has also led Christians to misread and misinterpret scripture.

4. The Gospels, as the rest of the New Testament, are products of developing traditions of the early Christian communities in which they were written. As such, they contain two types of information: history remembered and history metaphorized. While some of the information reported in the Gospels really happened, some of the tradition is not to be taken as literally true, for it represents the revised understanding of Christian communities following Easter.

5. The conceptual framework for understanding the process that led from encounter with Jesus of Nazareth to the revised theological understanding of Jesus as Christ may be viewed as a threefold process, beginning with (a) experience, then (b) metaphorical expression, and finally (c) conceptual formulation. Building on their experience of Jesus, the first Christians searched the Jewish scriptures for symbols that might relate to Jesus and help clarify his significance. Over time, these metaphors became the subject of intellectual reflection, conceptualized finally as doctrine.

6. Christianity originated as a Jewish eschatological movement. Like many Jews of their day, the first Christians embraced a doctrine of two ages, believing that the present evil age was giving way to the coming age of justice and peace. Jesus envisioned his mission in a quasi-prophetic manner, announcing God's coming reign while also envisioning in his own person and ministry the presence of that rule. For Jesus—as well as his earliest followers—the all-encompassing rule of God was near.

7. The concept of "resurrection," associated in Judaism with the coming of God's eternal rule on earth, became a reality for the followers of Jesus, who saw in the resurrection of Jesus the fulfillment of long-awaited eschatological expectations.

8. Once we understand the Judaism of Jesus, his followers, and of the apostolic church, the next step is to approach the Bible—both the Old and New Testament—from a Jewish perspective. The starting point for this understanding of scripture requires knowing how the Jewish people wrote sacred narrative. Beginning in the sixth century BC, following the return of the people of Judah from their exile in Babylon, there developed a need for commentary and reinterpretation of traditional texts in light of ever-present situations. This Jewish style of sacred storytelling, known as *haggadic midrash*, functioned to recontextualize already existing texts so as to enhance and enlarge their significance for a new cultural or historical setting. Such an approach was not concerned with historical accuracy but rather with meaning and understanding.

9. The same holds true for the Gospels. The first generation of Christians, the vast majority of whom were Jewish, undoubtedly saw *haggadic midrash* at work in the gospel tradition, recognizing certain Jewish antecedents present therein and noting that the authors were filtering their experience of Jesus through the traditions recorded in the ancient Hebrew scriptures. The underlying implication of this application of midrash is that many of the narratives in the Gospels were intended to be read metaphorically (as symbolic accounts fashioned to illustrate particular meaning) rather than as historical accounts. These texts were never intended to be understood literally in the first place.

10. Later, when the Gospels were read and interpreted by gentile Christians, this ancient methodology was unknown, and the Old Testament came to be valued only as a foreshadow of the life of Christ. As a result, gentile Christians came to view the Gospels narrowly, as the literal fulfillment of ancient expectations and as further proof of Jesus' divine nature. Losing the Jewish midrashic lens led to a distorting, anti-Jewish way of reading the Gospels that continued unchallenged for centuries.

Session 8

Rethinking the Resurrection
and the Afterlife

THIS SESSION EXAMINES CHAPTER 9 of *Beyond Belief*, a segment that addresses the centrality of Easter to Christianity.

Getting Started

Key Questions: Did the earliest Christians focus on the afterlife? What role did the resurrection of Jesus play in their understanding of eschatology?

Initial Assignment: Do you believe in life after death? How vital is this belief to how you live your life?

What really happened on Easter, and what does Easter mean for Christians? Is it possible to affirm the reality of the Easter experience without the necessity of literalizing the details of the resurrection moment? Did the loss of a Jewish haggadic perspective toward sacred stories result in a distortion of the intended message? Did gentile Christians misunderstand not only the nature of the Gospels and their portrayal of the life, death, and resurrection of Jesus but also misinterpret Paul's classic explanation of resurrection in 1 Corinthians 15? What was it that the gospel writers were trying to convey concerning the resurrection? What did "experiencing Jesus alive" mean to them?

A clue to the answers can be found in the intention of the gospel writers, whose symbolic language signaled they were neither writing history nor biography. They were trying to interpret a life-changing experience, but they could use only limited human words. The gospel writers signaled this weakness of vocabulary to their readers by exaggerating their language to the point at which their words became incongruous if understood literally. Once we admit the inadequacy of human language to describe the realm of the divine, we must address the inconsistencies present in the biblical texts about Easter. The discrepancies in these texts indicate that the core message of Easter is spiritual, not physical: Jesus continued to be experienced after his death, but in a radically new way, as a spiritual and divine reality.

As Christianity evolved, the evolution required metaphorical and conceptual development, a process akin to what modern theologians call "remythologization." During the following century, when the New Testament traditions took shape, Christian communities used a large number of metaphors or images, mostly drawn from the Hebrew Bible, to speak about Jesus and his significance. Over time, these metaphors produced a transformed perception of Jesus that led to the "canonical Jesus" of the New Testament and the "creedal Jesus" of later Christianity.

Gaining Momentum

1. How do you view life after death?

2. Belief in a literal bodily resurrection of Jesus has been held by many as a linchpin upon which Christianity stands or falls. Do you agree with this view? Support your answer.

3. Do you agree with Spong that the Gospels provide clues that support a spiritual rather than a literal understanding of key events in the life of Jesus, and that such events, while not literally factual, are nevertheless true for Christian believers. How, for Spong, can biblical events such as the resurrection be both true and non-factual?

4. Do you agree with the argument that Paul's understanding of resurrection in 1 Corinthians 15 is about a spiritual rather than a physical (bodily) resurrection? If so, how (and when) did the belief in Christ's physical resurrection arise?

5. In your estimation, does the concept of midrash augment or diminish the meaning of Jesus's resurrection?

6. If Jesus did not rise literally or physically, what other explanations can be given for the rise of Christianity and for the Church's Easter faith?

Going Deeper

An examination of John's Gospel, the last canonical gospel to be written and the most spiritual, teaches that eternal life is a present reality and not simply a longing for life after death (see, for example, John 3:36, where the present tense indicates that eternal life is here and now, for all who believe in Jesus). That a person's standing before God is determined not by a future resurrection but by the present relationship with Jesus is illustrated by John's account of the dialogue between Jesus and Martha in the story of Lazarus. In John 11:23 Jesus informs Martha that her brother will rise again. She thinks he is referring to the resurrection at the end of time and agrees with him (11:24), but Jesus corrects her. He is referring to possibilities in the present, not the future: "I am the resurrection and the life. Those who believe in me, even though they die, will live, and everyone who lives and believes in me will never die" (11:25–26).

How does this interpretation impact the Christian doctrine of the afterlife? With this perspective in mind, examine the entire gospel of John to see if you can find additional insights to substantiate this de-eschatologized understanding of the afterlife.

The Essentials: Key Points from Chapter 9
of *Beyond Belief*

1. Jesus was crucified. That is history. All else in the Christian creeds is but commentary on the meaning of what Jesus' life meant and means.

2. Easter is central to Christianity. Whatever Easter was, it had incredible power. It revolutionized the theology of a group of Jewish people so dramatically that the world has never been the same.

3. While it is impossible to know what really happened, since the loss of a Jewish haggadic perspective toward sacred stories undoubtedly resulted in a distortion of the intended message, it is clear that the gospel writers did not believe they were writing history or biography. They were trying to interpret a life-transforming experience, not capture a literal description of an objective event.

4. Symbolic language is everywhere present in the story of Jesus' life, including the birth narratives, the accounts of miracles, and the tales describing the final events in Jesus' death and resurrection.

5. To explain belief in the resurrection, it is helpful to return to the threefold process described earlier to construct theological meaning: (a) experience comes first, then (b) metaphorical expression, and finally (c) conceptual formulation. In the beginning was the experience of the earliest believers, then the phase in which they introduced metaphors and images as a way to speak of the resurrection and its significance, and finally doctrine. It took time for Christians to conceptualize their experience of the death and resurrection of Jesus. The further removed in time the crucifixion and resurrection accounts were from the experience itself, the more embellishment occurred. During the third phase, the mystery and wonder of the first and second phases were replaced by objective accounts and physical proofs. Acknowledging the process that utilized metaphor, legend, midrash, and tradition enables readers of the New Testament to understand the transition from experience to meaning.

6. The process of conceptualizing the resurrection was aided by the Jewish apocalyptic framework, based on the expectation that the present age was about to end. Many Jews believed this end would be presaged by the arrival of the messiah and the resurrection of the dead. The first Christians saw Jesus as the decisive sign (as the "first fruits") of that expected apocalyptic resurrection (1 Cor. 15:20).

7. Christians who ponder the meaning of the death and resurrection of Jesus often associate it with the concept of "eternal life," envisioned as a future reality. But eternal life need not be confined to the future. When Jesus was quoted in John's gospel as saying that he had come to give others life, and give it abundantly (10:10), he was divulging his grandest teaching: we already have eternal life. Eternal life, according to this understanding, is present to the extent that believers are in communion with that life-enhancing power of love called God.

Session 9

Reconciling Science and Religion

THIS SESSION EXAMINES CHAPTERS 10 and 11 of *Beyond Belief*, a segment that addresses how science and religion relate. Are they compatible? Can they be harmonized? Can one believe in God in an age of science? These questions constitute one of the most fascinating, important, and challenging controversies of our time.

Getting Started

Key Question: In what ways does science impact religion?

Initial Assignment: Select a question among those listed in the second paragraph of page 149 of *Beyond Belief* that commands your attention. Where would you start in constructing an answer?

Chapter 10 examines three contemporary models whereby science and religion can be related: (1) opposition (conflict); (2) separatism (contrast); and (3) engagement (consonance).

Within the opposition camp two antagonistic viewpoints attempt to provide an ultimate explanation of reality: (1) scientific materialism ("scientism"), in which scientific evidence provides ultimate truth, and (2) biblical literalism, in which religious faith provides ultimate truth. While both represent opposite ends of the theological spectrum, they share characteristics in common. Both camps claim that science and theology make rival claims about the same domain, namely the history of nature, so that one must choose between them. Both misrepresent science. Scientific materialists start from science but end up making broad philosophical claims. Biblical literalists, on the other hand, move from theology to make claims about scientific matters. Both fail to respect the differences between the two disciplines.

The separatist approach views science and religion as totally independent and autonomous realms, each with its own domain and its characteristic methods. As distinct jurisdictions, neither should meddle in the affairs of the other. Because there should be no real competition between evolutionary science and religion, the separatist approach appeals to many theological camps within Christianity. While separatism is a good starting point for analyzing the relation between science and religion, it is ultimately unsatisfactory, for its theological adherents end up with a distorted view of religion. For some Christians, nature is devalued and the gulf between God and the world remains vast. Other Christians end up privatizing and interiorizing religion, limiting God to the realm of selfhood and rendering nature devoid of religious significance. Such an anthropocentric framework offers little protection against the exploitation of nature. Relegating science and religion to watertight compartments also rules out the possibility of constructive dialogue and mutual enrichment.

Despite the presence of distinctive functions and attitudes in religion that have no parallels in science, there are also functions and attitudes in common. Ian Barbour identifies four methodological parallels for testing and evaluating theories or beliefs: (1) agreement with data, (2) coherence or consistency with other accepted theories or beliefs, (3) comprehensiveness of scope, and (4) future promise (fertility). Whereas scientific concepts and theories rely on corroboration from particular observations and experimental data, the data for a religious community consist of the distinctive experiences of individuals plus the stories and rituals of a religious tradition. If the theological task is systematic reflection on the life and thought of the religious community, this should include critical assessment according to the fourfold set of criteria that religion shares with the scientific community. Engagement maintains that science and religion, while logically and linguistically distinct, cannot be easily compartmentalized; science is not as objective, nor religion as subjective, as some assume. Since truth cannot contradict itself, scientific and religious truth must be reconcilable.

Chapter 11 presents a hierarchical model to depict the relations between theology and the sciences. Physics, the study of the simplest building blocks of reality, appears at the bottom. The rest of the sciences are located in order above physics, representing the fact that they study increasingly complex systems. Adopting this model, the Anglican theologian and biochemist Arthur Peacocke proposes that theology be considered a science and then places it at the top of the entire hierarchy, since theology involves the study of the most encompassing system of all: God in relation to both the natural world and human society. This model reconciles the best insights of the Opposition and Separatism viewpoints while also affirming the Engagement model, since it recognizes that theology cannot be isolated from the rest of knowledge.

The relation between theology and the sciences is much like the relation between one science and another. Each science employs its own proper language and subject matter and provides a relatively autonomous description of reality. Yet each science can learn from its neighbors. Thus theology provides a relatively autonomous description of reality, yet has some things to learn from the sciences and some things to teach them as well. While some may object to classing theology among the sciences, theology operates much like a science. It has its own proper data—from history, revelation, and the cumulative experience of the church—and its doctrines are comparable to theories in the sciences, rationally justified by their ongoing ability to explain the data.

Religion and science are ways of thinking and instruments of knowing. While less than perfect, they are the best we have, and it is important that they find ways to complement one another. Liberally educated scientists and people of faith are encouraged to value and utilize select tools from their collective toolkit, including intuition and imagination; self-criticism and an inquiring mind; reverence and a sense of awe; humility and support for contradictory perspectives; experimentation; democracy and the free exchange of ideas; and elegance in methodology and simplicity in solution.

One insight that historians and philosophers of science have given to our generation is that theories and models constructed by scientists to make sense of natural phenomena remain provisional. The final description of the universe has yet to be devised, the full potential of science yet to be realized. In this endeavor, the role of religion is invaluable. Reductionism brings science into conflict with religion, just as biblical literalism inevitably leads religious people to reject aspects of science. At their best, science and religion are indispensable and equally necessary; as Albert Einstein famously remarked: "Science without religion is lame, religion without science is blind."

Gaining Momentum

Chapter 10

1. If the notion of evolution is determined to be compatible with Christian teaching, what is it about Darwin's version of evolution that has been so disturbing? Explain your answer.

2. Explain how it might be possible, as stated on page 156 of *Beyond Belief*, that Darwin's theory of evolution could actually enhance one's understanding of God.

3. Using the concept of fertility (see page 157 of *Beyond Belief*), describe how religion might contribute greater promise to science. Likewise, describe how science might contribute greater promise to religion.

4. Reflecting on your own religious experience, which of the categories described on pages 158 and 159 of *Beyond Belief* best cohere with your own religious experience? Explain your answer.

5. If entropy is a defining aspect of the cosmic story, how can that story be said to contain promise? Explain your answer.

Chapter 11

1. If the meaning of scripture is mediated through human interpretation, how does this impact your understanding of the authority of scripture?

2. Discuss the relation between the concept of God's "Two Books" and the notion that "all truth is God's truth"? What value do you find in these affirmations?

3. What merit does "the principle of accommodation" hold for the reading and interpretation of scripture?

4. Comment on the validity of the statement found on page 174 of *Beyond Belief*: "It is reductionism that brings scientists into conflict with religion, just as biblical literalism inevitably leads religious people to reject aspects of science."

5. Of the seven qualities noted on pages 175–179 of *Beyond Belief*—intuition, self-criticism, awe, humility, experimentation, democracy, and elegance—which, in your estimation, provide the greatest prospect for religiously minded and scientifically guided individuals in their common quest for truth? What other qualities would you add to this list?

Going Deeper

In chapter 4 of *Religion and Science* Ian Barbour presents four models that conceptualize the relationship between science and religion: conflict, independence, dialogue and integration. Which of these models do you find most promising? Which model most realistically describes the current relationship between these disciplines? For additional insight, consider reading Barbour's book or John Haught's *Science and Religion*.

The Essentials: Key Points from Chapters 10 and 11 of *Beyond Belief*

Chapter 10

1. In the past, the biblical accounts of creation and salvation provided Christians a cosmic setting in which individual life had significance. Since the Enlightenment, the Christian story has had diminished effectiveness for many people, partly because it seemed inconsistent with the understanding of the world in modern science.

2. Darwinian evolution, while not necessarily troublesome to religious people, forces Christians to rethink their understanding of reality. Its theory of human descent from lower forms of life, its notion of natural selection, and its emphasis on randomness in evolution appear to diminish if not eliminate the role of God, the uniqueness of humans, and the need for Christ.

3. Scientific skeptics marvel at the tenacity of traditional religious institutions in the face of evolution, viewing theology as a puzzling anachronism. Many religionists respond by ignoring the claims of Darwin altogether. As it turns out, Darwin's ideas may considerably deepen and widen our understanding of God.

4. Utilizing the notion of "a hierarchy of explanations," it is possible to view theology as having a legitimate claim in the explanation of life, though not necessarily the exclusive or ultimate explanation.

5. While all religions view religious experience as primary, they all interpret this experience by a set of concepts and beliefs. The assessment of beliefs within religious communities and the principles used to support scientific theories follow similar criteria, although the criteria are applied somewhat differently. They include (a) agreement with data, (b) coherence

with other accepted beliefs, (c) scope of the primary data, and (d) fertility (future promise of beliefs, theories, and experiences). In addition to experience, religious data include stories and rituals. Religious narratives inform us about ourselves and our communities. They are recalled in liturgy and acted out in ritual.

6. No question in science or religion strikes more directly at the heart of human concern than that of cosmic purpose. According to the British physicist James Jeans, modern science depicts a universe hostile to life and consciousness, one destined for death at the hands of entropy. Entropy, as he understands it, suggests that the universe is either indifferent or hostile to life, since all human aspirations are doomed to final frustration.

7. The engagement model assimilates the scientific story of the universe with the story of promise embedded in traditional Western religious consciousness. If the universe is viewed as essentially storyless, it is not difficult to envision life as pointless. But if the cosmos is fundamentally a story, then one can posit a "point" to the story, including the plausibility of purpose for human existence. In this hopeful setting, even entropy can be given a new reading, for entropy guarantees that the cosmic story will avoid endless repetition while yielding unanticipated novelty. In a scientific age, a promissory universe makes room for religious optimism and hope.

Chapter 11

1. It has long been recognized that the sciences can be organized into a hierarchy, with physics at the base, then chemistry, biology, psychology, and sociology. Higher sciences permit study of increasingly more complex organizations or systems.

2. While the hierarchical model is well accepted among scientists and philosophers, there has been a longstanding debate concerning the issue of reducing each science to the one below, thereby reducing all reality to the laws of physics. Those who support a perspective known as "nonreductive physicalism" propose instead a nonreducible hierarchy of levels in nature consisting of the inorganic, organic, mental, social, ethical, and spiritual. This view criticizes the reductionists for their overly mechanistic and atomistic view of nature, arguing that organizational patterns and wholes are genuinely significant in their own right and not mere aggregates of elementary particles. Atoms, for example, are real, but so also are humans.

3. Many scientists working at a variety of levels are recognizing that analysis and reduction do not yield a complete or adequate account of

the natural world. In simple terms, to understand an entity, one has to consider not only its parts but also its interactions with the environment. This means that both "top-down" and "bottom-up" approaches are needed to account for the natural world.

4. In such a complex universe, does theology belong in the hierarchy of sciences? The Anglican theologian and biochemist Arthur Peacocke proposes that it does and that it be placed at the top, since its subject matter is the most encompassing system possible—God in relation to everything else. Theology's place atop the hierarchy is not due to its primacy of value or to its authority, however, but solely to its subject matter.

5. To defend the integrity of science and religion, church theologians have promoted the concept of "Two Books," the Book of Nature and the Book of Scripture. When the language of the latter seemed to contradict that of the former, theologians invoked the principle of accommodation, encouraging readers of scripture to recognize that ancient biblical authors were not making revelatory statements about the nature of the universe but were simply describing the phenomena of nature in a way understandable and accessible to ordinary and unlearned people. The Two Books concept remains a fruitful metaphor for understanding the relationship between biblical and secular knowledge.

6. Our knowledge of the universe remains incomplete, for the sum of human knowledge about the natural world is always increasing. For this reason, science and philosophy consider their models to be provisional, welcoming ongoing research while acknowledging that additional knowledge and new information provide the impetus and necessity to construct new theories to explain nature. Likewise, theologians and religious scholars should remain open to further insight and information, viewing their doctrines, models, and explanations as provisional.

7. Theologians remind us that the purpose of the Bible is not to provide timeless or definitive teaching about science or nature but rather to point to Jesus Christ. All else is secondary.

8. Religion and science are instruments for knowing and connecting, but each is imperfect. They are at their best, however, when they share a common toolkit. The qualities they must share include imagination, self-criticism, awe, humility, experimentation, democracy, and elegance. When science and religion work together, the inhabitants of the world will benefit, for such cooperation, based on the free and open exchange of ideas, will lead us all forward to a more promising future.

Session 10

Rethinking Evolution
and Human Uniqueness

THIS SESSION EXAMINES CHAPTERS 12 and 13 of *Beyond Belief*, a segment that introduces the topic of evolution, the overarching paradigm that governs the modern scientific worldview. It tackles the most troubling aspect of evolution for many Christians, namely the notion that humans have evolved from earlier life forms.

Getting Started

Key Question: If humans evolved from non-human life forms, are they spiritually distinct among living species?

Initial Assignment: Biblical religions teach that humans are made in the image of God. What meanings does this concept convey? Are any of these views compatible with human evolution?

Chapter 12 provides an overview of the theory of evolution, examined cosmically and biologically. Much of the information is well known and accepted by scientists around the globe, yet widely ignored or opposed by a large segment of the American public. The widespread ignorance, illiteracy, or misconception associated with the theory of evolution in the U.S. is, unfortunately, often attributable directly to religion. Many Christians in America brazenly disbelieve in biological evolution and take offence at the concept. Part of the problem also lies with the politics of local educators across the nation. Many children in our schools and churches are being taught that one cannot believe in both God and evolution for evolution is an atheistic philosophy contrary to the Bible.

This ignorance affects not only knowledge of life on this planet but also knowledge about the nature of the cosmos. We live in an evolving and expanding cosmos that began some 13.7 billion years ago and that remains unfinished. The universe story needs to be told, embraced, and celebrated, for in its story we find our own, the unfolding story of the human race. The story of evolution, properly told, contains truths essential to the wellbeing of our planet and all its inhabitants. It is a fascinating story, one we can no longer willfully ignore or misunderstand.

Chapter 13 considers the nature of human beings in greater detail, including the implications of human evolution for the biblical view that humans are created "in the image of God." This introduces the matter of dualism, a divisive issue in our culture. Many people assume humans are made of two parts: a physical body and a nonmaterial mind or soul. Increasingly, scientists, philosophers, and biblical scholars are calling this theory into question. A non-dualistic approach is more consistent with science and also more consistent with biblical thought. This "nonreductive physicalist" account also fits nicely with the hierarchical model described in chapter 11. As we go up the hierarchy of levels from physics and chemistry to biology—from nonliving to living—we see that life is a result of the special *organization* of nonliving matter rather than of the addition of any new substance such as a vital force. Similarly, as we go from the non-human to the human level, entities such as a soul or mind need not be added.

The chapter examines two themes central to creationist theology: the assumption of an original perfection of creation and the assumption of original sin. These doctrines have had a long history in Christian thought, but upon further examination they appear to be based more on shallow biblical literalism than upon general Christian teaching regarding sin and redemption.

Gaining Momentum

Chapter 12

1. Broadly speaking, do you agree with the presentation in this chapter concerning cosmic evolution? What do you find most intriguing and most perplexing? Where in this story, if at all, would you locate God's presence?

2. Broadly speaking, do you agree with the presentation in this chapter concerning biological evolution and the human story? What do you find

most intriguing and most perplexing? Where in this story, if at all, would you locate God's presence?

3. Regarding the scope of biological evolution, is it possible scientifically to believe in microevolution but not in macroevolution? Explain your answer.

4. How would you respond to those who argue that Darwin and ensuing Darwinian biologists claim that humans are descended from apes?

Chapter 13

1. Throughout church history, various explanations have been given to explain the existence of the human soul and to validate its existence. Which do you find most helpful? Are explanations of the soul primarily heuristic (helpful and explanatory), examples of what religious scholars call "pious fictions"?

2. How does science explain human consciousness? Do you believe it will be possible some day for technicians to create a machine or robot that can duplicate human consciousness? Why or why not?

3. Can morality ultimately be reduced to a function of the human brain? How does the story of Phineas Gage help us answer that question?

4. What is meant by "original sin"? In your estimation, what are the merits of this doctrine? Should that doctrine be understood and applied metaphorically or literally? What limits does science impose upon a literal understanding of this doctrine? Are the insights of Patricia Williams helpful on this topic?

5. Given the biblical emphasis on the original goodness of the created order (see Genesis 1), is it possible for human nature to change from essentially good to essentially corrupt (fallen)? Explain your answer.

Going Deeper

Go online and find websites associated with Young Earth Creationism and Intelligent Design. What are their central teachings and what are their primary concerns? On what points do Young Earth Creationist and Intelligent Design advocates agree and where do they disagree. Do you find their arguments attractive or convincing? Why or why not?

The Essentials: Key Points from Chapters 12 and 13 of *Beyond Belief*

Chapter 12

1. It is important, in studying science in general and evolution in particular, that we identify antiscientific bias in religion but also antireligious bias in science. Some scientists exceed the limits of their discipline by expanding science into a materialistic philosophy that seeks to dispense altogether with religion and belief in God. Evolution needs to be understood and evaluated as science, not as philosophy.

2. When scientists describe the universe today, they understand it far differently than did Isaac Newton and his eighteenth century successors. Newton's universe was infinite in scope and static by nature, following natural laws established by God. Today's scientists describe the universe as expanding and unfinished, with an explosive start some 13.7 billion years ago and a probable ending not yet in sight. Our own sun is a star formed about 5 billion years ago, and our earth became a planet about 4.6 billion years ago.

3. The cosmos should not be viewed as static and fixed but as an unfolding drama whose story is still being written. People might speculate about its future on the basis of what science has learned about the past, with some confidence that the processes by which nature has unfolded over time are likely to continue. Nevertheless, the future remains open, whatever one might speculate.

4. The earth contains a vast and biologically diverse array of plants and animals, perhaps as many as twelve million species, found in every nook and cranny on the planet. The fossil evidence indicates that 90 percent of all species ever alive are now extinct. If scientists are correct in their claim that this astonishing diversity is the outcome of evolutionary processes, this means that all living things are interrelated, having descended from one or more common ancestors. Charles Darwin called this process "descent with modification," a phrase that accurately describes what scientists today call "macroevolution."

5. Biological evolution is a broad unifying scientific concept. It consists of a large array of proposed mechanisms that draw on a wide range of observational data from a great many related fields of science. As a unifying concept, evolution provides a core of solidly established fact and theory

combined with a number of related theories and hypotheses.

6. Hominids, of which humans are the only surviving species, belong to the order of primates, which includes monkeys, chimpanzees, and gorillas. In addition to obvious skeletal similarities, humans and other primates also share such traits as nails instead of claws, opposable thumbs, erect postures, relatively large and complex brains, lengthened periods of maturation, and habitation in year-round social groups containing members of both sexes. At some point in the past the family of hominids, including the human species, developed traits that set its members apart from other primates. These include straight-knee bipedalism, increased cranial height and capacity, and dental changes leading to reduced projection of the face. And humans developed, alone among primates, the abilities of language, abstract and symbolic thought, and other capacities of culture and technology.

Chapter 13

1. If one believes that the creation is a kind of "Book of Nature," then the scientific data that support the conclusion that humans have evolved biologically cannot simply be dismissed. Those who believe that the Bible is infallible in all areas of knowledge take the accounts in Genesis as presenting scientific and historical truth about origins and dismiss the conclusions of science concerning humans as speculative and incomplete. Other Christians (called concordists) accept the evidence for an ancient earth and for hominid precursors to Homo sapiens while at the same time maintaining that the figure of Adam in Genesis is historical.

2. There are better ways to understand the figures of Adam and Eve. If one applies the principle of accommodation, it becomes evident that the biblical writers were depicting the origin of humankind in a way that was comprehensible to the people of their time. Such an interpretation raises a different and more fundamental question: How does one understand theologically the meaning of imago dei in an evolving humanity? The starting point for this discussion is to note that the expression "image of God" is not meant to be taken literally. In the Bible it is often associated with thought and reason and the capacity to act freely, meaning that humans are spiritual and moral beings. The New Testament extends the notion to the saving work of Christ, who restores the divine image given in creation and disfigured through sin.

3. Do humans have souls, or are they solely physical beings, the result of the atoms and molecules of physics, biology, and chemistry? Increasingly our culture is developing an understanding of the human person as purely physical. Much of this view comes from science as well as from philosophical arguments. Virtually by definition a religion that gives prominence to souls is bound to clash with a theory like Darwinism, which is bound to be thoroughly reductionistic.

4. The word "soul" has had different meanings throughout church history. In the Hebrew scriptures, the word translated "soul" didn't mean what later Christians often meant by soul. In most cases "soul" is simply a way of referring to the whole living person. The New Testament usage is more complicated, leading to four current theories about the makeup of humans: (a) dualism (that humans are composed of two parts, an eternal soul and a perishable body); (b) reductive materialism (that humans are solely physical beings); (c) holistic dualism (that humans are composed of two parts, termed "body" and "soul," both being essential and intended to function harmoniously); and (d) nonreductive physicalism (that humans are solely physical organisms, but that their brain and neurological system provide moral and even spiritual capacities). The first two are incompatible with Christian teaching, while the latter two are compatible. Though holistic dualism has been the most common position through church history, nonreductive physicalism remains close to the ancient Hebrew conception of the person, while maintaining the holistic view of the person found in both the Old and New Testaments.

5. Nonreductive physicalism fits nicely into modern psychological theory, which views human consciousness as dependent upon the special organization of the parts as found in the brain and not upon some nonmaterial construct such as "mind" or "soul." Order is what genetic "code" is all about, and the same holds true of the brain. The very crux of Darwinian explanation of the distinctiveness of humanity is that humans are ordered and thus can function in ways not possible for other animals.

6. There is a growing body of data on regions of the brain responsible for various mental and emotional capacities. This research has allowed for the localization of a vast array of cognitive functions, including speech, color, facial recognition, and emotion. The case of Phineas Gage, who suffered brain trauma that resulted in the loss of moral function, is instructive. His intellectual capacities were undamaged, but he lost the appetite for good, which in Thomistic language meant he lost his appetite for God.

While developments in neuroscience can never prove there is no soul, one can look at localization studies and say that functions of the soul are surprisingly well-correlated with certain brain functions. In the current climate, the concept of the soul seems an unnecessary complication.

7. According to creationists, there was no death before the fall of Adam and Eve, for death came into the world as a result of Adam's sin. While this doctrine—called "original sin"—has had a long history in Christian thought, it has not been universally accepted. In fact, the idea is based more on a shallow biblical literalism than upon general Christian teaching regarding sin and redemption. In addition, scientific evidence indicates that living creatures had died long before the advent of humankind. There are a number of Christians in the sciences who once accepted strict creationism but later abandoned it without losing their faith, for what creationists are defending is a particular interpretation of scripture, not scripture itself.

8. If one is prepared to accept a metaphorical interpretation of the Adam and Eve story, a biological understanding of "original sin" emerges. As Darwinians have shown, the struggle for existence often involves self-interest, if not outright selfishness. Original sin as part of the biological package comes with being human. According to sociobiologists, the influence of genes, the environment, and the misuse of human freedom adequately account for the origin of sin and the problem of human evil. There need be no contradiction between evolution and a realistic notion of original sin. The notion of original sin, in this sense, reminds us of our human incapacity to save ourselves from this state of affairs. The need for a savior, central to Christianity, is in no way diminished by recent evolutionary knowledge.

9. This is why evolution is potentially such good news for theology. It enables theologians to subordinate the understanding of the "history of salvation" as restoration—the recovery of a primal perfection of being—to the far more accurate and fulfilling understanding of the history of salvation as transformation—the novelty and surprise of an unfinished universe.

Session 11

Rethinking Evolution and Cosmic Purpose

THIS SESSION EXAMINES CHAPTER 14 of *Beyond Belief*, a segment that discusses the topic of teleology, noting that Darwinism challenges traditional understandings of design in the universe.

Getting Started

Key Question: If the cosmos evolved randomly, can we speak about our lives having meaning and purpose?

Initial Assignment: Throughout much of Western philosophical and religious history, the teleological argument for God—based on arguments supporting design in the universe—seemed convincing in supporting the existence of a creator or intelligent designer. Which arguments for design, cosmic and human, do you find most damaging for Darwinian evolution? Which arguments do you find to be least convincing? Support your answer.

Four topics have been central in the theological debate over evolutionary theory: the challenge to scripture, to the status of humanity, to ethics, and to design. Concerning the latter, the most persistent arguments affirmed by proponents of theistic design include (1) the fitness of organisms to their environments and the apparent design of their organs to serve specific purposes; (2) the unique role of humans in the created order and in relation to God; (3) the view that social norms and human values are reflective of divine will and should not be reduced to naturalistic explanations such as the survival of the fittest; (4) divine sovereignty over nature; (5) the Genesis account of creation; and (6) the pseudo-religious phenomenon in science, whereby scientists and philosophers like Carl Sagan use concepts drawn from science as substitutes for what are essentially religious categories.

Proponents of Darwinism cite two broad objections against theistic notions of creation, including the corollary view that purpose and design were built into the fabric of nature from the start: (1) the antiquated perspective of the biblical writers and (2) the overwhelming biological evidence of human adaptation. While science possesses a valid and purely naturalistic explanation of design, evolutionary biology is only one level of a whole hierarchy of explanations needed to understand in depth the story of life. Theology can be part of such a hierarchy of explanations.

Gaining Momentum

1. Darwin's theory of natural selection is said to build on three ideas: (a) random variations, (b) the struggle for survival, and (c) the survival of the fittest. Which of these three do you find most essential to the theory and therefore most convincing? Why?

2. If you were to construct a dialogue or debate with Carl Sagan (see page 218 of *Beyond Belief*), how would you evaluate his "naturalistic religion"? With which of his concepts would you concur and with which would you disagree? Explain your answer. How would the matter of "boundary questions" be helpful in your critique of his perspective?

3. In your estimation, can (or should) science ever be used as a replacement for religion? What, for you, are the most persuasive arguments against scientism?

4. Discuss the merits of the "via media" compromise that arose after the publication of Darwin's Origin and why modern contributions in the field of biblical studies challenge intellectually such a position (see the discussion on pages 220–223 of *Beyond Belief*).

5. Discuss the merits and problems associated with the existence of a closed canon (the process of inscripturation) for modern Christians (see the discussion on pages 222 and 223 of *Beyond Belief*).

6. Critique (or assess the merits of) the arguments marshaled by critics of supernatural theism against the existence of God (see page 225 of *Beyond Belief*).

7. Which arguments against design (see the discussion on pages 228–232 of *Beyond Belief*) do you find best support the claims of evolutionary

biology in dismissing the Christian doctrine of creation? Support your answer.

8. Do you find Haught's notion of "promise" in the universe (see pages 233 and 234 of *Beyond Belief*) as a way to explain God's presence and involvement with the world to be more scientifically and intellectually attractive than the older idea of "design"? If you agree, explain how his argument promotes the hierarchy of explanations (including those of evolutionary biology) needed to understand most fully the story of life.

Going Deeper

One of the goals of our study is to look for possible "consonance" between science and religion. As noted above, four topics were central to the theological debate that followed the publication of Darwin's *Origin of Species* in 1859. Construct an answer that suggests consonance between science and:

- the nature and authority of scripture and its interpretation (note the discussion on pages 219–223 of *Beyond Belief*);

- the status of humanity (note the discussion in chapter 13 of *Beyond Belief*);

- the moral nature of humanity and social Darwinism (note the discussion on pages 216 and 217 of *Beyond Belief*);

- the question of design, cosmic and human (see the arguments pro and con in chapter 14 of *Beyond Belief*).

For additional perspective read Kenneth R. Miller's penetrating study *Finding Darwin's God* (1999), written by an eminent professor of biology who is also a Christian.

The Essentials: Key Points from Chapter 14 of *Beyond Belief*

1. Ever since Darwin published his *The Origin of Species* in 1859 and *The Descent of Man* in 1871, Christians have been divided over the implications of his thought. While some Christians find the theory of natural selection threatening to their faith, others have no objections. A topic central to the debate that followed was Darwin's challenge to design.

2. One reason why Christians have objected to Darwinian evolution is that it spoils the popular argument for the existence of God. The argument

for design in the universe is predicated on the teleological argument for the existence of God. In 1802 William Paley provided a persuasive treatment of teleology in the universe. The universe, according to Paley, is like a watch, and a purposeful instrument like a watch cannot come into existence on its own. It requires the existence of an intelligent designer. Such an argument is flawed, however, as demonstrated by the philosopher David Hume, who pointed out the vulnerability of arguments like Paley's on the basis that the universe does not exhibit sufficient design to support the argument. Conceding that the universe does show a great deal of order, he demonstrated that there is disorder and evil as well.

3. Theists can respond to Darwin's theory in at least two ways: (a) they can argue that the process of natural selection is the way in which a divine designer might work out his purpose for the world, or (b) they can look beyond biology and locate marks of design elsewhere in the universe, such as in the apparent "fine tuning" of the natural laws and physical constants.

4. Many Christians cite conflict with Genesis as a major reason for rejecting Darwin's theories. This conflict can be minimized and even eliminated by recognizing that the Bible contains various kinds of literature, each deserving to be read accordingly. The original readers would not have read the Genesis stories literally, and modern readers are encouraged to give attention to the human character of the biblical texts.

5. There are two broad arguments used to dismiss the biblical notion of creation: (a) the antiquated perspective of the biblical period and (b) biological evidence of human adaptation. The limitations of the biblical perspective are well known. They include the concept that biblical authors and their audiences lived in highly superstitious times. Additionally, scholars note the rhetorical nature of the New Testament, which indicates that this material was written to persuade and instruct believers rather than to record actual history.

6. Of the arguments against the existence of God, two are considered persuasive by critics of supernatural theism: (a) the biblical God is inactive today and (b) the biblical God is immoral. This deity not only punishes sinners with natural disasters, but declares all humans to be guilty and judges them with death, condemning many to eternal damnation.

7. In addition to disagreement with biblically based reasoning, a second source of argumentation for dismissing the biblical doctrine of creation comes from evolutionary biology. As Richard Dawkins notes,

physiological vestiges are reminders that evolutionary history is written in the bodies of all living creatures, constituting persuasive evidence for the occurrence of evolution. Organisms created by an intelligent designer would surely be nearly perfect, demonstrating evidence of purposeful design. The many imperfections of the human backbone, the presence of an appendix, feet poorly constructed for walking and running, the improper drainage of sinuses, and even eyes prone to optical errors, all are explainable fully by evolution. Evolution tinkers, improvises, and cobbles together new organs out of old parts. A true designer would not work that way.

8. The same applies to the larger economy of nature, including the suffering caused by plagues, pestilence, and parasites. A beneficent designer might seek to minimize suffering in nature, but what we find is the opposite: suffering among wild animals so appalling that it makes no sense in a world designed and maintained by a beneficent creator. The same holds true for speciation. The fossil record shows that 90 percent of all species that ever lived have become extinct. This can be explained by a random, undirected process like evolution, but not by an intelligent creator.

9. If we are going to speak honestly and intelligently about God after Darwin, we must do better than simply polish up old design arguments. John Haught proposes the concept of "cosmic promise." Starting with the Augustinian suggestion that a creator has richly endowed the universe, from its opening moments, with the potential for evolving toward complexity, Haught suggests that God "seeds" the universe not with design but with the promise of novelty and complexity that eventually becomes alive and conscious, at least here on earth. The key point is that evolutionary biology, widened by cosmology, has made us realize that we live in an unfinished universe. The physical universe is a work in progress, and religions, firmly embedded within nature itself, are continuous with this evolutionary responsiveness.

Session 12

Conclusion

THIS SESSION EXAMINES THE Conclusion and Epilogue of *Beyond Belief*, which affirms a panentheistic perspective as compatible with evolutionary biology and with faith in the biblical God of self-giving love. Such a view allows not only for randomness and uncertainty in the universe but also actually anticipates an evolving universe.

Getting Started

Key Question: Can process theology be attractive to the majority of Christians? (Consult appendix A of *Beyond Belief*)

Initial Assignment: Having concluded this study, write a brief statement indicating how this experience has enabled you to grow in your faith and in your understanding of the relationship between faith and reason.

The ultimate source of both order and novelty in evolution is "God." Such a God, according to process theology, is not interested simply in maintaining the status quo but desires a universe always open to new ways of becoming. As the source of novelty, God's power is persuasive rather than coercive.

Arguing that the God of biblical religion is a God of persuasive love, the source of novelty, and the stimulus to adventure, process theology embraces evolution as indispensable, for it helps recover a richer and more biblical sense of God. Assuming the validity of such an argument, the purpose of humanity, when situated in the context of cosmic evolution, would be to carry forward in whatever way possible the general creative aim of the universe toward deeper and wider beauty. A lively awareness of the general cosmic aim toward beauty provides humans a rich context in which to cultivate individual lives.

The key point for this understanding of religious faith is to acknowledge that belief in doctrines is not central. Speaking from personal experience, the author indicates that to encounter God one must go beyond belief to faith, to the joy of "unknowing." While faith cannot overcome intellectual uncertainty, it can overcome doubt about the significance and worth of one's life.

Gaining Momentum

1. Having concluded this study, what do you find to be the merits of the Engagement position regarding science and religion? Are you optimistic that greater numbers of traditional Christians might commit to this perspective? What problems remain to be worked out?

2. Can panentheism be attractive to the majority of Christians? Why or why not?

3. Discuss the merits and limitations of process theology (consult appendix A in *Beyond Belief*).

4. In response to the understanding of evil mentioned on page 240 of *Beyond Belief*, does Haught's "evil of monotony" enhance or trivialize our understanding of evil? Support your conclusion.

5. In his book *Resurrection: Myth or Reality?* Bishop Spong defines God as "the love that creates wholeness." Evaluate the merits of this understanding of God in light of two comments from *Beyond Belief*: (a) In the preface of *Beyond Belief* (page xiii) the author notes that of the nine realizations which inform his belief and behavior, the greatest is "the experience of love in the universe." (b) In the epilogue of *Beyond Belief* (page 243) the author maintains that "the chief end of man is to experience fully the unfolding cosmic adventure called Love."

6. Chart out your understanding of what is meant (and not meant) by the biblical assertion that (a) God is love (1 John 4:16) and that (b) love is the fulfillment of the whole law (Gal. 5:14; Rom. 13:8; Matt. 22:36–40).

Going Deeper

Read Deepak Chopra's *How to Know God* (see the summary in appendix B of *Beyond Belief*) and answer the following questions: (a) which stage best describes your current understanding of and relationship with God? (b) which stage best describes your spiritual goal?

The Essentials: Key Points from the Conclusion and Epilogue of *Beyond Belief*

1. The way of Engagement suggests that science and religion share a common origin in the mysterious human desire to know. It is because of their shared origin in this fundamental concern for truth that they can never be allowed simply to go their separate ways.

2. Living in a post-Darwinian universe, where evolution is a fact of life, does not demand that we give up the idea of God. Rather it asks that we think about God in a fresh way. For a growing number of Christians today, evolution is a helpful and even a necessary ingredient in our thinking about God. It comes down to this: If there exists a loving God who is intimately related to the world, we should expect an aspect of indeterminacy in nature. The reason is simple; love typically operates not in a coercive but in a persuasive manner. It allows the beloved—in this case the entire created cosmos—to remain itself, though in such a way as to imply intimacy rather than abandonment. Viewed in this light, it would be very difficult for us to reconcile the religious teaching about God's infinite self-giving love with any kind of universe other than an evolving one.

3. In the light of randomness, impersonality, and cruelty of natural selection, a version of Christian thought called "process theology" is addressing the issue of purpose in the universe. The philosopher Alfred North Whitehead noted that all of nature is in process of becoming. To account for nature's restlessness, he insisted, we must postulate a principle that explains not only the order we observe in nature but also the novelty that emerges in evolution. The ultimate source of both the order and the novelty in evolution is "God." God, according to process theology, is not interested simply in maintaining the status quo but desires a universe forever open to new creation. God, therefore, influences the cosmos by holding out before it, at every instance, new ways of becoming.

4. In an evolutionary cosmos, what do the notions of "evil" and "sin"

mean in process theology? According to Haught, there are two forms of evil: (a) the evil of disorder (examples of which are suffering, war, famine, and death) and (b) the evil of monotony. This latter evil clings to trivial forms of order or refuses to open up to what is fresh and emerging. Whatever else we may understand by "sin," in an evolving universe it includes our refusal to participate in the ongoing creation and renewal of the cosmos.

Epilogue

1. According to Søren Kierkegaard, the Danish existentialist philosopher, one becomes a Christian by means of a leap of faith, by which he meant the commitment of one's entire being. Though doubt can never be completely overcome, the leap is not irrational if it is impelled by one's heart, nurtured by one's will, and fueled by one's faith. One leaps, not because there is a shortage of evidence, but because one recognizes the domain of the heart.

2. Whereas Christians of his day focused on the content of religious faith, Kierkegaard sought not intellectual certainty but existential authenticity, focusing not on the content of Christianity but rather on what it means to be a Christian. For Kierkegaard, one does not become Christian by coming to know something one did not previously know. Rather, one becomes a Christian as one becomes human, by embarking on a path. It would be quite normal to start on the path without ever reaching the goal, since one never actually becomes a Christian; one simply strives to become one.

3. The key point for this understanding of religious faith is to acknowledge that belief in doctrines is not central, since they are themselves unprovable. Faith involves heart-knowledge, in addition to head-knowledge, the giving and committing of one's life to whatever we consider ultimate. Such living is "beyond belief."

Appendix A

James Fowler's Stages of Faith

Stage 0: *Primal Faith*—**(0 to 2 years):** This stage is characterized by early learning the safety of the environment. Under consistent nurture, children develop a sense of safety about the universe and the divine. Negative experiences (neglect and abuse) lead to distrust of the universe and the divine.

Stage 1: *Intuitive-Projective*—**(3 to 7 years):** This is the stage of preschool children in which fantasy and reality often are mixed together. However, during this stage, our most basic ideas about God are usually learned from our parents and/or society.

Stage 2: *Mythic-Literal*—**(mostly in school children):** When children become school-age, they start understanding the world in more logical ways. They generally accept the stories told to them by their faith community but tend to understand them in very literal ways. [A few people remain in this stage through adulthood.]

Stage 3: *Synthetic-Conventional*—**(arising in adolescence; ages 12 to adulthood):** Most people move on to this stage as teenagers. At this point, their lives have grown to include several different social circles, which they need to pull together. When this happens, a person usually adopts some sort of all-encompassing belief system. However, at this stage, people tend to have a hard time seeing outside their box, not recognizing that they are "inside" a belief system. At this stage authority is usually placed in individuals or groups that represent one's beliefs. [In this many people remain.]

Stage 4: *Individuative-Reflective*—**(usually mid-twenties to late thirties):** This is the tough stage, often begun in young adulthood, when people start seeing outside the box and realizing that there are other "boxes."

They begin to examine their beliefs critically on their own and often become disillusioned with their former faith. Ironically, Stage 3 people usually think that Stage 4 people have become "backsliders" when in reality they have actually moved forward.

Stage 5: *Conjunctive Faith*—(**mid-life crisis**): It is rare for people to reach this stage before mid-life. This is the point when people begin to realize the limits of logic and start to accept life's paradoxes. As they begin to see life as a mystery, they often return to sacred stories and symbols but this time without remaining in a theological box.

Stage 6: *Universalizing Faith*—(**enlightened stage**): Few people reach this stage; those who do, live their lives to the full in service of others without real worry or spiritual doubt.

Simplified Version by M. Scott Peck
(*The Different Drum*)

I. *Chaotic-Antisocial*—People in this stage are usually self-centered and often find themselves in trouble due to unprincipled living. If they do finally embrace the next stage, it often occurs in a very dramatic way.

II. *Formal-Institutional*—At this stage people rely on some sort of institution (such as a church) to give them stability. They become attached to the forms of their religion and become extremely upset when these are called into question.

III. *Skeptic-Individual*—Those who break with the previous stage usually do so when they start seriously questioning previously held values and beliefs. Frequently they end up non-religious and some stay here permanently.

IV. *Mystical-Communal*—People who reach this stage start to realize that there is truth to be found in both the previous two stages and that life can be paradoxical and mysterious. Emphasis is placed more on community rather than on individual concerns.

Appendix B

Discovering Your Personality
and Spirituality Type

WHILE THIS GUIDE MAKES no attempt to persuade you to join one or another organized religion or spiritual practice, it does provide, in this appendix, valuable tools for discovering your psychological type and then for matching your personality characteristics with one of four spirituality types identified by religious scholars and found in various faith traditions.

Discovering Your Personality Type

If you have never taken the Myers Briggs Type Indicator (MBTI), or if you need to verify your personality type, I recommend that you take the online version of the test.[1] But before you do, keep in mind that the MBTI is not really a test but a sorter of preferences in four categories. There is no "right" or "wrong" answer. In order to get accurate results, adopt a relaxed demeanor and remember that you are attempting to discover *your* preferred answer to each question, not what you or your parents or anyone else wished you preferred as an answer. Since humans are complex individuals, our preferences may vary from situation to situation. The MBTI reports preferences on four scales, each consisting of two opposite poles. The following exercise conveys what is meant by "preferences":

---

1. To find your type, go to www.humanmetrics.com and click on "Jung Typology Test" and then "Take Test." Either before or after taking the test, click on the Full Description link for clarification of the Jungian terminology and concepts. Once you have completed the 72 questions, click "Score It" at the bottom to obtain your results. The entire exercise will take 10 to 15 minutes. For further analysis and potential verification of your personality type, consult www.personalitypathways.com/type-inventory.html.

First, on the line below sign your name as you normally do;

_____

Now, sign your name again on the line below, but this time use your other hand;

_____

The first result was effortless and natural, the second awkward and unnatural. Similarly, according to the theory, everyone has a natural preference for one of the two opposites on each of the four MBTI scales. You use both preferences at different times, but not both at once and not, in most cases, with equal confidence.

At the conclusion of the test you will receive four letters, which comprise your personality type. They indicate the differences in people that result from

- where they prefer to focus their attention (Extraversion or Introversion)—E or I;

- the way they prefer to take in information (Sensing or Intuition)—S or N;

- the way they prefer to make decisions (Thinking or Feeling)—T or F;

- how they orient themselves to the external world (Judging or Perceiving) J or P.

These preferences produce sixteen different kinds of people, interested in different things and drawn to different fields. Each type has its own inherent strengths as well as its likely blind spots. Discovering one's personality type is extremely beneficial, for it influences career choices, marriage choices, learning style, spiritual journeys, theological understanding, and so much more.

For the moment, let's examine learning styles associated with each preference, since inclinations at this dimension impact choices at other cognitive, relational, and intuitive levels.

Extraverts	*Introverts*
Learn best when in action	Learn best by pausing to think
Value physical activity	Value reading
Like to study with others	Prefer to study individually
Prefer discussion	Prefer clear lectures
Sensors	*Intuitives*
Seek specific information	Seek quick insights
Observe specific facts	Use imagination to go beyond facts
Follow practical interests	Follow intellectual interests
Prefer step-by-step instructions	Create their own directions
Like hands-on experience	Like theories to give perspective
Trust material as presented	Read between the lines
Seek mentors who give clear teaching	Seek mentors who encourage independent thinking
Thinkers	*Feelers*
Want objective material to study	Want to relate to the material personally
Logic guides learning	Personal values important
Like to critique new ideas	Like to please instructors
Can easily find flaws in an argument	Can easily find something to appreciate
Learn by challenge and debate	Learn by being supported and appreciated
Want mentors who make logical presentations	Want mentors who establish personal rapport
Judgers	*Perceivers*
Like instructions for solving problems	Like to solve problems informally
Value dependability	Value change
Plan work well in advance	Work spontaneously
Work steadily toward goals	Work impulsively with bursts of energy
Drive toward closure	Stay open to new information

Using combinations of preferences also yields interesting results on the topic of learning styles. Combining the first two letters of your type reveals some interesting patterns. The first two letters show where you prefer to focus your attention and how you prefer to take in information. For example, ES types are usually more interested in the practical usefulness of learning, while IN types are usually more interested in abstractions and learning for its own sake. College samples of type distributions reveal widespread discrepancies between faculty and students in terms of teaching and learning preference. Whereas a majority of college faculty fall into the IN and EN categories, ES and IS types predominate among college students.

Using the second and last letters of one's type is also a useful way to think about learning style. The second letter (S or N) describes whether one prefers to focus on facts and reality (Sensing) or abstract concepts and theories (Intuition). The last letter (J or P) indicates whether one prefers to decide on that information quickly and then move on (Judging) or keep open to new information (Perceiving). College samples indicate that there are three times as many students who prefer Sensing and Perceiving as there are faculty with this combination. SP students prefer a flexible approach to factual material. Their NJ professors, on the other hand, prefer structure and theories. The SP students are more likely to view the facts themselves as more important than the theories and are less likely to want the facts organized according to some grand structure. No matter which preference combination one examines, however, it is clear that Sensing types will probably need to learn to cope with the Intuitive environment preferred by the majority of their professors.

This information, when applied to educational and liturgical settings, might presumably uncover a similar disconnect between academically trained clergy and laypersons on at least two fronts: (a) in terms of teaching and learning preference as well as (b) in terms of theological appreciation and understanding.

Typology and Spirituality

Each person is unique, with a distinct personality. Despite their uniqueness, individuals share personality traits, qualities, and preferences that can be defined and typed into distinct categories. That, as we have seen, is the premise upon which the MBTI is built. These insights have a remarkable correlation with spirituality, as we discover in the following typologies.

Richardson's Typology

Building on the insights of psychological type theory developed by Carl Jung and Isabel Briggs Myer, Peter Tufts Richardson notes that four different approaches to human spirituality emerge from the MBTI.[2] How we perceive the world and how we respond to it (how we judge) seems to be directly connected to the spiritual path we find most personally satisfying. Utilizing the principle that one's spirituality flows out of one's individuality,

2. His approach is described in *Four Spiritualities*.

Richardson locates the key to spirituality in the two middle letters of one's personality type. These cognitive pairs result in four possibilities: ST, SF, NT, and NF. One of these pairs defines each person's spirituality.

Richardson defines the four spirituality types and identifies mentors from different world religions for each journey:

ST—Journey of Works (Moses)

SF—Journey of Devotion (Muhammad)

NT—Journey of Unity (Buddha)

NF—Journey of Harmony (Jesus)

Richardson offers additional mentors for each spirituality type (see below), while describing qualities and patterns unique to each path.

STs are characterized by a *task-oriented spirituality*. ST youth are drawn to activities that are task-oriented, such as team sports. And often they will be leaders. They may help with chores around the house, but they are not particularly swayed by the desires of a parent. They learn by experience, wanting to discover things for themselves; they need to know why things are required and how they work. As teens STs divide into two groups: the freedom lovers (STPs) and the responsible ones (STJs), but all are oriented around well-defined institutions. When they grow up, STs become the realists, always in touch with the facts, unbiased, objective, accurate, paying attention to relevant details. They are skilled administrators, responsible, consistent, efficient, and analytical. The Journey of Works is practical and involves a lifetime of effort; people on this path like to follow procedures efficiently, often legalistically. Work is the means for meeting all obligations and responsibilities. It gives life dignity and results in solid citizenship. STs commit themselves to the building up and maintaining of institutions, reliably and loyally. They prefer direct, experience-based, often physical activities, working with their hands or otherwise directly in situations, trying out procedures to see what works best, often preferring technical tasks to those requiring people skills. They learn best on the job, noticing relevant details, collecting facts, and verifying them directly by the senses. They arrive at conclusions in a linear cause-and-effect way. Their opinions, based on their experience, will often be firmly held and based on common sense. A confusion of beliefs is intolerable for STs. They like to find a world in balance, with reliable structures that lead them toward the right way to go. For the Journey of Works, order and a clear message are essential conditions. Appreciating clear beliefs and reliable structure, they tend to be literalists and legalists in religion; commitment provides religion stability.

ST mentors include Confucius, Clement of Alexandria, Origen of Alexandria, Augustine, Ignatius of Loyola, Martin Luther, Brother Lawrence, George Washington, and Gandhi; biblical mentors include Ruth, Abigail, Martha of Bethany, and Peter.

SFs are characterized by an *experience-based spirituality*. SF youth make friends easily, avoid conflict, and desire to please. They thrive in well-structured environments and when expectations are clear. They need to be reassured when they are on the right track and rewarded for good behavior. As adults SFs are sensitive, loyal, and caring; they live responsibly as parents and citizens and are devoted to serving others in tangible ways. In the Journey of Devotion, living in the immediate present is central. Instead of the cosmic, the tangible task at hand is the focus. Details are important. Stressing continuity and propriety, SFs are traditionalists. In their communications they prefer anecdotes, stories, and tangible references to symbolic or abstract reasoning. Practical and interactive, they take a tactile, hands-on approach to the spiritual life.

SF mentors include St. Benedict, St. Francis, Julian of Norwich, John Wesley, and Ramakrishna; biblical mentors include Esther, Mary Magdalene, Nicodemus, Mary of Bethany, and John.

NTs are characterized by a *highly principled spirituality*. NT youth value their independence and tend to work hard to establish their competence in the challenges they decide to tackle. Uncomfortable with abstraction, they often ask why, and if the answers they receive are unsatisfactory, they may set out to improve upon them or else to rebel against arbitrary answers. As adults NTs tend to enjoy solving problems, love to exchange ideas, or stimulate new efforts. Searching for unifying solutions, they appreciate speculative theories that lead to intellectual clarity. In the Journey of Unity, the search for truth or the quest for perfection is often as satisfying as the conclusions reached along the way. NTs are foremost change agents and strategic planners. On account of their critical nature, they may be perceived by others, particularly SFs, as stubborn or uncooperative. Along with principles and truth, individuals on this path are also distinguished by vision and concern for social justice.

NT mentors include Socrates, St. Dominic, Thomas Aquinas, John Calvin, Albert Schweitzer, Dorothy Day, Martin Luther King Jr., Elie Weisel, Albert Einstein, and Ralph Nader; biblical mentors include Amos, Deborah, and Paul.

NFs are characterized by a *questing spirituality*. NF youth like to please the adults and peers in their lives. They can be easily crushed by disapproval or even indifference. They need regular affirmation from parents and teachers if their self-esteem and self-image are not to suffer. Because they see possibilities in the future (N) and like to gain approval from others, they often will prepare for careers and causes in response to adult mentors in their lives. NF youth are exceedingly idealistic. Their idealism is often unpredictable; some young men may overcompensate for their F by expressing their idealism in hostile ways. They are strongly represented among protestors for social issues. NF adults are enthusiastic and insightful, recognizing the personal needs of others. Idealists by nature, they always see a way to make life better. They have an ability to draw people into a discussion and to facilitate consensus-building for social harmony and good. NFs on a healthy track will regularly draw others toward their own best selves. The Intuitive proclivity for symbol and metaphor, combining with global vision for the wellbeing of the world, makes NFs inspired communicators of the ideal. Future-oriented and attuned to the big picture of life as a whole, people on the Journey of Harmony tend to focus more on possibilities than on concrete situations at hand. Their N nature is balanced, however, by their F side, which keeps them in touch with reality and keeps their utopian bent in check. Flexible and open to change, NFs see life as continual self-creating process, a quest toward selfhood. Their malleable natures exist to be formed and re-formed in ever more exquisite patterns of self-actualization. NFs seek increasing meaning and spiritual purpose in life.

NF mentors include Meister Eckhart, Teresa of Avila (also SF and ST), St. John of the Cross, Thoreau, Walt Whitman, Tagore, Thomas Merton, and George Fox (Quakers); biblical mentors include Abraham, Joseph, Miriam, and Mary (mother of Jesus).

Holmes's Typology

Urban Holmes, dean of the School of Theology at The University of the South in Sewanee, Tennessee from 1973 until his death in 1981, presents a helpful typology for the spiritual life in his insightful book *The History of Christian Spirituality*. It provides a tool and a method by which to conceptualize and name spiritual experience within a basic framework, particularly useful in helping to position one's own religious experience within the context of the experience of others.

Holmes suggests two appropriate ends for the spiritual life: a speculative spirituality that focuses on the illumination of the mind and an affective spirituality that focuses on the illumination of the heart. He further suggests two appropriate means toward those ends: a kataphatic means—an indirect way of knowing in which our relationship with God is mediated—and an apophatic means—a direct way of knowing, in which our relationship with God is not mediated.

Holmes calls his model the "Circle of Sensibility," and in it he delineates four styles of prayer, later configured as schools of spirituality. By "sensibility" he refers to the possibilities within individuals and communities as they seek to understand the experience of God and its meaning for our times. Holmes proposes the use of two intersecting lines placed within a circle. The vertical line creates a north-south axis, with Speculative (Mind or Intellect) at the north pole and Affective (Heart or Emotion) at the south pole. The horizontal line creates an east-west axis, with Kataphatic (God as Revealed: known through images) at the east pole and Apophatic (God as Mystery: known mystically) at the west pole. Below is an adaptation of his circle, divided into four quadrants. Each quadrant contains one of the four schools of spirituality, which he labeled "speculative-kataphatic" (Type I spirituality), affective-kataphatic (Type II spirituality), affective-apophatic (Type III spirituality), and speculative-apophatic (Type IV spirituality).

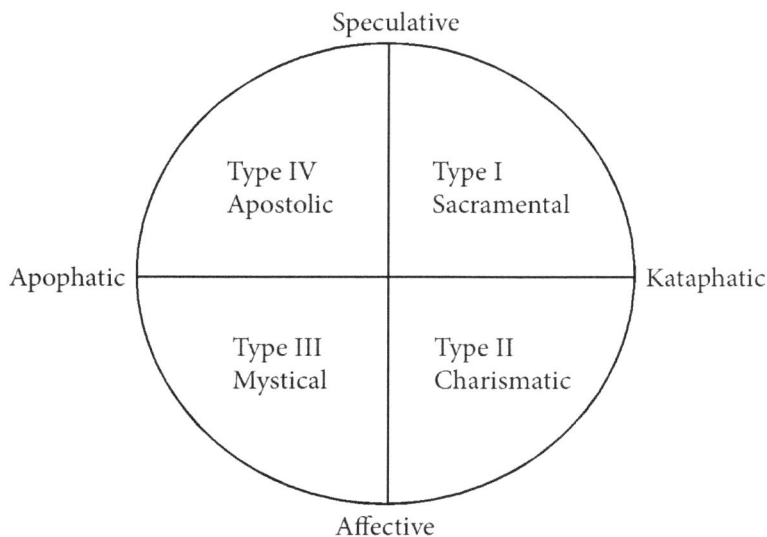

Speculative

Type IV
Apostolic

Type I
Sacramental

Apophatic

Kataphatic

Type III
Mystical

Type II
Charismatic

Affective

Type I spirituality, an intellectual "thinking" spirituality, has been identified as "sacramental." Its primary aim is to aid persons in fulfilling their vocation in the world. This spirituality favors what it can see, touch, and vividly imagine. Type II spirituality, a sensate, heartfelt approach to spirituality, has been identified as "charismatic." Its primary aim is to achieve holiness of life through personal renewal. Type III spirituality, which emphasizes being and direct experience of God, has been identified as "mystical." Its primary aim is union with the Holy, an unattainable goal, a journey that nevertheless continually impels the disciple onward. Type IV spirituality, a visionary, almost crusading type of spirituality, has been identified as "apostolic." Its primary aim is to obey God's will completely. Its major concerns are witness to God's reign and striving for justice and peace.

It is clear that Holmes's typology overlaps significantly with Jung's typology, as incorporated in the MBTI, and that it is compatible with Richardson's adaptation and analysis of the four spirituality types. In his description of the four "schools" of spirituality, Holmes cautions against excess, for each of these approaches appears subject to a distortion or natural "heresy." A heresy is a truth that goes too far, denying its countertruth.

Type I spirituality (the speculative-kataphatic approach) falls prey to the "heresy" of rationalism (*an excessive concern for right thinking* that leads to dogmatism) if it denies the validity or counterbalance of Type III spirituality (affective-apophatic), its diagonal (opposite) approach. Each approach should look to its diagonal spirituality for growth and balance. Type II spirituality (the affective-kataphatic approach) risks falling into the "heresy" of pietism, *an excessive concern for right feelings* that leads to emotionalism. Type III spirituality (the affective-apophatic approach) is subject to the "heresy" of quietism or isolationism, *an excessive concern for right internal experience* that leads to escapism or withdrawal; and Type IV spirituality (the speculative-apophatic approach) may fall into the "heresy" of encratism, *an excessive concern for right behavior* that leads to moralism. Each approach, then, needs to be held in tension with its opposite.

The understanding of spirituality provided by these typologies results in great benefit to one's spiritual identity as well to the level and nature of engagement with one's worshipping community. For example, from this fountain flow insights concerning one's approach to worship, prayer, and meditation.

Type I spirituality produces theological reflection and crafts position papers. Its practitioners are analytical, apprehending theology as doctrine.

Divine guidance comes chiefly through scripture and sermons. Worship is orderly and patterned. Reading is central to this spirituality. Prayer in this quadrant is word-based and thought-out, whether aloud or silent. Theological discussion is common with this type, but if not balanced with other activities, can lead to one-dimensional "head trips."

Type II spirituality uses an entirely different spiritual "vocabulary" in expressing its heartfelt intuition. Since experience must be shared, its adherents often emphasize evangelism and personal transformation, sometimes of a sudden type. Witnessing, testimonials, and especially music mark congregational worship. Theologically this approach stresses immanence over the transcendence of God. Friendship with Jesus and an outpouring of the Spirit provide signs of God's presence in life. Type II prayer is often word-based but stated extemporaneously. Worship is full of feeling, energy, and bodily freedom of expression that Type I worship generally lacks. African-American churches have this capacity for spontaneity and enthusiastic worship. Not only in the U.S. but also worldwide, many Christians formerly concentrated in Type I mainline denominations are now leaving and, where they seek corporate worship, are moving to congregations that represent more affective (charismatic) types of worship.

Type III spirituality is dominated by contemplative prayer, the purpose of which is not to fill or express the mind as to free the mind. The goal is to empty the self from all distractions so as to be fully receptive. Classic Christian congregational approaches may be found in Quaker worship, which silences the senses to create empty space, and Eastern Orthodox worship, which makes use of the senses as a means of eliminating their influence. While Orthodox utilize icons, music, and incense as vehicles for the mystery spiritually present but hidden, Quakers eliminate sermons, clergy, and sacraments altogether, emphasizing hearing rather than speaking. This form of worship attracts people who are by nature contemplative, introspective, intuitive, and inner directed. Representatives of this approach, often uncomfortable with organized religion, find simple life styles appealing. Historically, Type III spirituality has pushed the frontiers of theology in the West, providing rich fodder for predominantly Type I spirituality.

Type IV spirituality, which combines mystic experience with an intellectual mode of gathering data, attracts single-minded visionaries with a deeply active spirituality. Practitioners of this mode of spirituality often care less than do others about affiliation with organized religion, certainly less than those in types I and II. Their aim is to obey God. Theirs is a courageous idealism that takes responsibility for change, creating a passion for transforming society. Type IV practitioners equate prayer and theology with action. What other spirituality schools might consider a response to prayer (obedience), this school considers as actual prayer. Disciples on this path often participate in marches and rallies and seek to serve in the Peace Corps or locally in organizations such as AmeriCorps. Taking as their motto the words of Jesus in Matthew 25:40: "Truly I tell you, just as you do it to one of the least of these . . . you do it to me," they associate worship and prayer with the presence of God, particularly evident in situations of human need.

As we sort for personality and spirituality types, we need to keep in mind that no two people are identical, even when they share the same characteristics. Some show a clear preference for a particular function, others a moderate or even a weak preference. So persons who share the same characteristics may, in fact, be quite different. Individuals who sort into the same spirituality type, based on their perceiving or judging functions, are further distinguished by their other cognitive functions: their life attitudes (E or I) and their life orientations (J or P). Further, all of us can learn to use the opposite functions. These psychological types, like the schools of spirituality, are not boxes into which we can place people. They are simply typologies that can help us better understand ourselves and others, especially those who differ from us.

Many texts attempt to find correlation between the Myers-Briggs categories and the four schools of spirituality. If one assumes that the four poles correlate with the four middle functions—the speculative pole with T, affective with F, kataphatic with S, and apophatic with N—the results place STs in the speculative-kataphatic (Type I) quadrant, the SFs in the affective-kataphatic (Type II), the NFs in the affective-apophatic (Type III), and the NTs in the speculative-apophatic (Type IV). While attractive for its simplicity, this solution has its detractors, including John Westerhoff, longtime professor at Duke University Divinity School, who supports Jung's contention that only the stronger of the two middle traits (our dominant function) is a useful indicator of behavior (see the discussion above on "type dynamics"). According to this insight, four categories are available: T, S, N, and F. From this perspective, the schools of spirituality and personality types configure like this:

- the speculative-kataphatic (Type I) quadrant = S
- the affective-kataphatic (Type II) quadrant = F
- the affective-apophatic (Type III) quadrant = N
- the speculative-apophatic (Type IV) quadrant = T

Jung offers another insight. He suggests that in our lives we need to differentiate between work and leisure; if our personality needs are met in our work, we will seek their opposite in our leisure. This is another way of affirming that in our lives—physically, emotionally, and spiritually—as we move back and forth from dominant quadrants to diagonal quadrants, we will discover beneficial pathways for personal growth.

Gaining Momentum

1. On the basis of your MBTI type, identify how you perceive (acquire information) and how you judge (process information).

2. On the basis of your MBTI type, identify the characteristics of your preferred learning style.

3. On the basis of your spirituality type, identify additional mentors for your faith journey.

Going Deeper

Acquire a copy of Peter Tufts Richardson's *Four Spiritualities* (1996) and read the chapter related to your spiritual journey: (a) NT: Journey of Unity (chapter 4); SF: Journey of Devotion (chapter 5); ST: Journey of Works (chapter 6); NF: Journey of Harmony (chapter 7).

Bibliography

Achtemeier, Paul J. *The Inspiration of Scripture: Problems and Proposals*. Philadelphia: Westminster, 1980.

Allen, Diogenes. *Christian Belief in a Postmodern World: The Full Wealth of Conviction*. Louisville, KY: Westminster John Knox, 1989.

Armstrong, Karen. *The Bible: A Biography*. New York: Grove, 2007.

———. *The Case for God*. New York: Anchor, 2010.

———. *A Short History of Myth*. New York: Canongate, 2005.

Barbour, Ian G. *Religion and Science: Historical and Contemporary Issues*. New York: HarperSanFrancisco, 1997.

Borg, Marcus J. *The God We Never Knew*. New York: HarperSanFrancisco, 1998.

———. *The Heart of Christianity: Rediscovering a Life of Faith*. New York: HarperSanFrancisco, 2003.

———. *Meeting Jesus Again for the First Time*. New York: HarperSanFrancisco, 1995.

———. *Reading the Bible Again for the First Time*. New York: HarperSanFrancisco, 2002.

———. *Speaking Christian*. New York: HarperOne, 2011.

———, and N. T. Wright. *The Meaning of Jesus: Two Visions*. New York: HarperSanFrancisco, 2000.

Chopra, Deepak. *How to Know God*. New York: Three Rivers, 2000.

Darwin, Charles. *On the Origin of Species by Means of Natural Selection*. London: John Murray, 1859.

Dawkins, Richard. *The God Delusion*. New York: Houghton Mifflin, 2006.

Erikson, Erik. *Childhood and Society*. New York: Norton, 1963.

Foster, Richard J. *Celebration of Discipline: The Path to Spiritual Growth*. New York: Harper & Row, 1978.

Fowler, James W. *Stages of Faith*. New York: Harper & Row, 1981.

Fox, Matthew. *Original Blessing*. Santa Fe, NM: Bear & Co., 1983.

Haught, John F. *Deeper Than Darwin: The Prospect for Religion in the Age of Evolution*. Boulder, CO: Westview, 2003.

———. *God After Darwin: A Theology of Evolution*. Boulder, CO: Westview, 2000.

———. *God and the New Atheism*. Louisville, KY: Westminster John Knox, 2008.

———. *Responses to 101 Questions on God and Evolution*. Mahwah, NJ: Paulist, 2001.

———. *Science and Religion: From Conflict to Conversation*. Mahwah, NJ: Paulist, 1995.

———. *What is God? How to Think About the Divine*. Mahwah, NJ: Paulist, 1986.

Holmes, Urban T. *The History of Christian Spirituality*. New York: Seabury, 1980.

Lawrence, Gordon. *People Types & Tiger Stripes*. Gainsville, FL: Center for Application of Psychological Type, 1979.

Keirsey, David, and Marilyn Bates. *Please Understand Me: Character & Temperament Types*. Del Mar, CA: Prometheus Nemesis, 1978.

Bibliography

Miller, Kenneth R. *Finding Darwin's God: A Scientist's Search for Common Ground Between God and Evolution*. New York: Perennial, 1999.

Murphy, Nancey. *Reconciling Theology and Science*. Kitchener, Ontario: Pandora Press, 1997.

Myers, Isabel Briggs, with Peter B. Myers. *Gifts Differing: Understanding Personality Type*. Palo Alto, CA: Davies-Black, 1980.

Niebuhr, H. Richard. *Christ and Culture*. New York: Harper & Row, 1951.

Peck, M. Scott. *The Different Drum*. New York: Simon & Schuster, 1987.

Polkinghorne, John. *Belief in God in an Age of Science*. New Haven, CT: Yale University Press, 1998.

——. *One World: The Interaction of Science and Theology*. Princeton, NJ: Princeton University Press, 1987.

——. *Quarks, Chaos and Christianity: Questions to Science and Religion*. New York: Crossroad, 1996.

Richardson, Peter Tufts. *Four Spiritualities*. Palo Alto, CA: Davies-Black, 1996.

Ross, Diana Butler. *Christianity After Religion: The End of Church and the Birth of a New Spiritual Awakening*. New York: Harper & Row, 2012.

Ruse, Michael. *Can a Darwinian be a Christian?* Cambridge: Cambridge University Press, 2001.

Sagan, Carl. *The Demon-Haunted World: Science as a Candle in the Dark*. New York: Random House, 1995.

Schneider, Robert J. "Science and Faith: Perspectives on Christianity and Science." No pages. Online: http://community.berea.edu/scienceandfaith/default.asp.

Schulweis, Harold M. *For Those Who Can't Believe*. New York: HarperPerennial, 1995.

Schumacher, E. F. *Small Is Beautiful: Economics as if People Mattered*. New York: Harper Perennial, 2010.

Spong, John Shelby. *Eternal Life: A New Vision*. New York: HarperOne, 2009.

——. *Liberating the Gospels: Reading the Bible with Jewish Eyes*. New York: HarperSanFrancisco, 1997.

——. *Resurrection: Myth or Reality?* New York: HarperSanFrancisco, 1994.

——. *The Sins of Scripture*. New York: HarperOne, 2006.

——. *Why Christianity Must Change or Die*. New York: HarperOne, 1999.

Tattersall, Ian. *Becoming Human: Evolution and Human Uniqueness*. New York: Harcourt Brace and Co., 1998.

Walls, Andrew F. *The Cross-Cultural Process in Christian History*. Maryknoll, NY: Orbis, 2002.

——. *The Missionary Movement in Christian History*. Maryknoll, NY: Orbis, 1996.

Vande Kappelle, Robert P. *Beyond Belief: Faith, Science, and the Value of Unknowing*. Eugene, OR: Wipf & Stock, 2012.

Whitehead, Alfred North. *Science and the Modern World*. New York: Free Press, 1967.

Williams, Patricia A. *Doing without Adam and Eve: Sociobiology and Original Sin*. Minneapolis, MN: Fortress, 2001.

.

www.ingramcontent.com/pod-product-compliance
Lightning Source LLC
Chambersburg PA
CBHW071101090426
42737CB00013B/2422